Civil War Generals

AN ILLUSTRATED ENCYCLOPEDIA

★

The Civil War Society

Civil War Generals

AN ILLUSTRATED ENCYCLOPEDIA

INCLUDING NAVAL AND OTHER
MILITARY HEROES OF THE CIVIL WAR

★

The Civil War Society

GRAMERCY BOOKS
New York

This 1999 edition is published by Gramercy Books,™
an imprint of Random House Value Publishing, Inc.,
201 East 50th Street, New York, New York 10022
by arrangement with The Philip Lief Group, Inc.,
130 Wall Street, Princeton, NJ 08540.

Gramercy Books™ and design are trademarks of
Random House Value Publishing, Inc.

Random House
New York • Toronto • London • Sydney • Auckland
http://www.randomhouse.com/

Printed and bound in the United States of America

Photographs courtesy of the National Archives and the Library of Congress

Designed by Helene Wald Berinsky

Library of Congress Cataloging-in-Publication Data

Civil War Society's encyclopedia of the Civil War. Selections.
Civil War generals : an illustrated encyclopedia / the Civil War Society.
p.   cm.
"Originally published in a larger edition entitled The Civil War Society's
encyclopedia of the Civil War, 1997"—T.p. verso.
ISBN 0-517-20288-3
1. Generals—United States—Biography—Encyclopedias.   2. Generals—Confederate
States of America—Biography—Encyclopedias. 3. United States. Army—Biography—
Encyclopedias.   4. Confederate States of America. Army—Biography—Encyclopedias.
5. United States—History—Civil War, 1861-1865—Biography—Encyclopedias.
6. Generals—United States—Biography—Pictorial works. 7. Generals—Confederate
States of America—Biography—Pictorial works. 8. United States. Army—Biography—
Pictorial works. 9. Confederate States of America. Army—Biography—Pictorial works.
10. United States—History—Civil War, 1861-1865—Biography—Pictorial works.
I. Civil War Society.   II. Title.
E467.C582   1999
973.7'03—dc21   98-33253
CIP

Originally published in (and excerpted from) a larger edition entitled
The Civil War Society's Encyclopedia of the Civil War (1997)

8 7 6 5 4 3 2 1

Civil War Generals

AN ILLUSTRATED ENCYCLOPEDIA

★

The Civil War Society

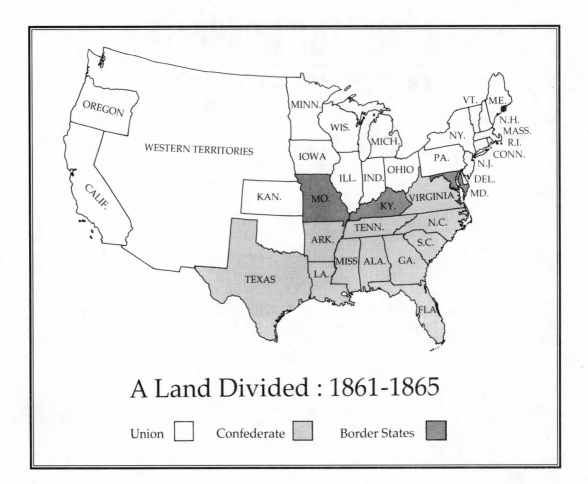

A Land Divided : 1861-1865

Union ☐ Confederate ☐ Border States ☐

Anderson, Robert
1805–1871

A West Point graduate who was severely wounded while serving with General Winfield Scott in the Mexican War, Anderson commanded Federal troops at Fort Sumter when asked to surrender the garrison to Confederate soldiers on April 14, 1861, marking the official beginning of the Civil War. Although sympathetic to slavery, Anderson was deeply loyal to the Union. For his brave actions at Fort Sumter, Abraham Lincoln promoted him to the rank of brigadier general on May 15, 1861. He took command of the Department of Kentucky and later of the Department of the Cumberland.

He retired in 1863, but returned to Fort Sumter in 1865 after it was recaptured to raise the Union flag before a respectful crowd. Anderson died in Charleston, South Carolina, in 1871.

Banks, Nathaniel Sarttle Prentiss
1816–1894

It seemed to have been the fate of Major-General Nathaniel S. P. Banks to step into the shoes of other men whose fame has overshadowed his own. Born into a middle-class mill-town family in Waltham, Massachusetts, Banks was required to leave school at a young age and work in his father's cotton mill; not deterred by this, Banks became a self-educated man, teaching himself Latin and sharpening a talent for public speaking. He also taught himself Spanish, and is probably the first American to state that such a skill would someday be important, given the proximity of the United States to countries whose people spoke that language. By the time he was approaching his fortieth year, Banks had been a member of the Massachusetts state legislature for five years under five different party affiliations. He was an ardent Free-Soiler who opposed the repeal of the Missouri Compromise and proclaimed to be a firm opponent of slavery. On the strength of this stand he moved into the Congress of the United States, and in 1856 declined nomination to the office of president. The following year, he successfully ran for governor of his home state—one of the first candidates in the Commonwealth's history to actually travel through the state campaigning on his own, a strategy which enobled him to defeat a long-term incumbent.

By the outbreak of the war, Banks had retired from his gubernatorial term. He was living in Chicago, where he had succeeded George B. McClellan as president of the Illinois Central Railroad. He immediately volunteered for service himself and was commissioned a Major-General of volunteers. Assigned to the department of Annapolis, Banks played a crucial role in preventing the

Maryland legislature from voting in favor of secession; he was then transferred to the Shenandoah Valley in the aftermath of the disastrous defeat of Union forces at Manassas (First Bull Run) on July 21, 1861, where he replaced the incompetent General Robert Patterson as commander of that department. Banks did not fare much better there, however, as a haphazard approach to reassignment of troops left him with an inadequate number of men to defend the pivotal valley town of Front Royal. Outnumbered two to one and facing the seemingly indomitable Stonewall Jackson, Banks lost Front Royal to the Confederates on May 23, 1862, and could see but one course open to him: immediate withdrawal and retreat. He fled before Jackson's superior forces in a running battle all the way to Winchester, Virginia, and with the Confederates on his heels Banks forced a crossing of the Potomac at Harpers Ferry. Upwards of three thousand of his men were taken prisoner, and he lost more than two hundred more in casualties, depleting his undermanned force to under seven thousand soldiers.

Smarting under the embarrassing defeat, Banks got a chance to avenge his honor less than three months later when, assigned to Union General John Pope in the Army of Virginia, he was ordered to attack the enemy at Cedar Mountain the moment the Confederates made any move whatsoever. On August 9, 1862, the Confederates moved—and Banks' men attacked with such violence that two divisions of Stonewall Jackson's left flank were driven from their superior position before the reserve under A.P. Hill could be brought up. Unfortunately two of Banks' com-

manders were wounded in action, leaving their regiments leaderless. Banks' personal command of the art of tactics was somewhat lacking; he was unable to make good on the initial success of his attack, and when the Federals were forced to retreat during Hill's counterattack, Pope denied he had ever ordered Banks to attack in the first place. The Joint Committee on the Conduct of the War looked into the matter and exonerated Banks, passing the blame back where it belonged, as the report said, "Of course, the order should not have been given."

Banks was briefly transferred to command of the defenses of Washington, D.C., before being detailed to succeed General Benjamin Butler as commander of the Department of New Orleans, where Butler had proven disastrously unpopular. Making do with the little he had—less than twenty thousand men effectively ready for offensive maneuvers—Banks gained creditable success in aiding General U.S. Grant in the task of reopening the Mississippi River. In late May 1863, during the attempt to take Port Hudson, Banks put black troops into the action by virtue of what he called their "utmost daring and determination." Laying seige to Port Hudson, Banks and his men endured a month and more of bombardment and a gallant but unsuccessful attempt to storm the garrison on June 13. Less than a week after Grant's victory at Vicksburg, on July 9, 1863, Banks forced the unconditional surrender of Port Hudson at last, removing "the last obstruction to the free navigation of the Mississippi River."

The remainder of 1863 was not good to Banks. Slow and difficult military advances, coupled with problems with the civilian population of his department, gave him all manner of trials; possibly in part due to the unpopularity of the previous commander, there was even an attempt on Banks' life. He tried instituting voting reforms in Louisiana and set up an alternative government for the state. Then early in 1864, Banks was called upon to assist General Grant in his Red River Expedition—which proved to be an unmitigated disaster, for which Grant attempted to blame Banks. With the government in Washington eager to see some substantive advances in Texas and Louisiana, Grant, Banks, and Admiral David Dixon Porter were ordered to make assaults upon Shreveport. Nearing his objective, Banks encountered stiff Confederate resistance at Sabine Crossroads on April 8, 1864, and was routed. The next day there was a vicious fight at Pleasant Hill, which ended in a bloody draw. With no supplies of food, water, or ammunition forthcoming, Banks was forced to withdraw; in addition, Admiral Porter's fleet was almost left marooned when the Red River suddenly and uncharacteristically receded from its usual April floodstage. They were barely rescued in time by an inspired piece of engineering, in which a swiftly constructed series of dams enabled the ships to float free of the shallows. Grant suddenly withdrew nearly half of Banks' effective fighting force for service elsewhere in the campaign, and on May 13, Banks was forced to give up Alexandria, Louisiana. Peremptorily replaced by the arrival of General E. S. Canby, Banks would later be blamed for the failure of the expedition by a majority opinion of the Joint Committee, with

only one member attempting to point out Banks could not possibly have foreseen the Red River's natural, if disastrously timed, behavior. Subsequent appraisal of the situation, however, is more likely to blame the fact that none of the commanders involved in the expedition "had the right to give an order to another," thus making communication between them difficult and pointless.

Banks was honorably mustered out of service several months after the final surrender of the Confederate armies, and resumed a life of political service. He was elected to complete the unexpired term of Republican Congressman D. W. Gooch—the member of the Joint Committee who had sought to defend him—when Gooch passed away, and Banks remained in the House of Representatives from the Thirty-ninth through Forty-second Congresses. Before the end of his final congressional term Banks became seriously ill, and returned to Waltham, Massachusetts, where he died in 1894.

Beauregard, Pierre Gustave Toutant
1818–1893

A poor relationship with Jefferson Davis kept P.G.T. Beauregard, one of the Confederacy's first war heroes, from receiving the top commands his talents and victories merited. The natty Creole general from Louisiana, an exuberant man with a hot temper, graduated second in his class at West Point, supervised dredging the mouth of the Mississippi River as the army's chief engineer in New Orleans, and ran unsuccessfully for mayor of the city. Appointed superintendent of the U.S. Military Academy in January 1861, Beauregard was dismissed within five days for his vocal pro-secessionist stance.

He soon entered the Confederate army and was assigned to demand the surrender of Fort Sumter in Charleston Harbor from his former West Point artillery instructor, Robert Anderson. Igniting the Civil War with his bombardment and almost bloodless capture of the Union-held citadel in April, Beauregard was idolized throughout the South. Three

months later, he commanded infantry forces in Virginia, and though technically outranked by Joseph Johnston, devised much of the Confederate strategy for the First Battle of Bull Run. An elaborate offensive he modeled on Napoleon's Austerlitz campaign did not come off, but a far simpler counterassault routed the Federals and won the South a stunning victory in the war's first major engagement.

Clashing with Jefferson Davis for not proceeding on to attack Washington, he was dispatched from Virginia to serve under Albert Sidney Johnston in the Western theater. In April 1862, Beauregard, despite some misgivings, coordinated the advance on Union forces sta-

Beauregard, before the Battle of Pittsburgh Landing: "I will water my horse in the Tennessee River or in Hell before night."

tioned at Pittsburgh Landing, Tennessee, and took over command in the ensuing Battle of Shiloh when Johnston was killed during the first day's fighting. Prematurely telegraphing Richmond of his imminent victory, he was forced to retreat to Corinth, Mississippi, the following day. One month later, Beauregard evacuated Corinth, strategically avoiding a disastrous confrontation with a far larger oncoming Union force. Davis, however, saw it as a grave setback and, when Beauregard went on sick leave, replaced him with Braxton Bragg. Returning to Charleston to head the defense of the Atlantic coast, Beauregard successfully repulsed numerous Union land and sea assaults on the port city for the next year and a half.

He was sent back to Virginia in the spring of 1864, where he stymied two critical Federal offensives: he halted a Union advance on Richmond in May when he cornered Benjamin Butler's army on the Bermuda Hundred peninsula; and held off Northern attacks on Petersburg the following month with a minuscule 2,500-man force until Robert E. Lee arrived to reinforce the vital rail center. His contributions still not properly recognized, Beauregard was assigned a vague administrative post in the West that fall, but was again called on to serve as Joe Johnston's second-in-command in the hopeless attempt to halt William T. Sherman's 1865 march through the Carolinas.

After the war, Beauregard, who had also designed the Confederacy's famed "Southern Cross" battle flag, declined military commissions from Romania and Egypt, and returned to New Orleans, where he took up the railroad business and ran the Louisiana state lottery.

Bragg, Braxton
1817–1876

Personally disliked by practicallyeveryone in the Confederacy, General Braxton Bragg displayed both tactical genius and fatal indecision on the battlefield. His Civil War career, highlighted by the brash but failed invasion of Kentucky, was marked by brilliantly planned campaigns that nearly all ended in disaster with thousands of troops slaughtered needlessly.

Born in Warren County, North Carolina, on March 22, 1817, Bragg graduated fifth in his West Point Class of 1837. Appointed lieutenant of the artillery, he served in Florida during the war with the Seminoles until 1843, then served on the frontier until the Mexican War. His gallant conduct at the battle of Monterery earned him a brevet to major; at Buena Vista, where he fought with Zachary Taylor, he was breveted twice for meritorious conduct. Bragg was commissioned colonel and then major general in the militia in early 1861.

During the first summer of the Civil War, Bragg commanded the coast between Pensacola and Mobile and was promoted to major general of the Regular army in September. Ordered to join the Army of the Tennessee, Bragg served under Albert Sidney Johnston as chief of staff and led the Confederate right flank at the battle of Shiloh. Both Confederate and Union troops displayed an enormous lack of discipline during this early and bloody battle; Bragg developed a low opinion of volunteer soldiers after his experience here. His abuse of troops in order to instill discipline was legendary. One private

General Braxton Bragg

wrote home that "He loved to crush the spirit of his men. . . . The more hangdog look they had about them the better." The fact that he suffered from severe migraines and other illnesses on the battlefield may help explain his disposition.

Nevertheless, his attributes as an able strategist and organizer outweighed—at least temporarily—his personal shortcomings. In June 1862, he earned a promotion to commander of the Confederate Army of the Mississippi, replacing Pierre T. Beauregard. Bragg immediately began to plan his Kentucky campaign—the first invasion of the North by the Confederacy—involving a two-prong attack by his troops and those of Major General E. Kirby Smith. Surprising the Union by taking the initiative, Bragg moved into

Kentucky in late August from posts in Tennessee, capturing two important garrisons (Kirby Smith taking the Union garrison at Richmond on August 30; Bragg's troops capturing Munfordville on September 17).

Just as suddenly, however, Bragg seemed to lose his nerve. Instead of consolidating his gains with military action, Bragg lost time by going to Kentucky's capital, Frankfort, to install a secessionist government and set up a recruitment effort. These actions allowed a now alarmed Union to send troops to stop the invasion of this important border state. Within three weeks, Major General Don Carlos Buell's Army of the Ohio had raced northward with nearly 50,000 men.

On October 7, 1862, the Federals moved against the Confederates at Perryville. Bragg, who had miscalculated Buell's intentions, had sent a division to Frankfort, leaving him with just 16,000 men, who were further decimated during the long day of battle that ended in a virtual stalemate with heavy losses on both sides. Realizing that he was outnumbered by the full force of Buell's Army of the Ohio, Bragg decided to retreat. Luckily, his opponent shared his indecision and lack of will; Buell missed his opportunity to pursue the Confederates and crush Bragg's forces once and for all.

Just five months after the start of his bold campaign, Bragg was back in Tennessee in front of Union forces at Nashville, with the bulk of his army in camp at Murfreesboro. On December 31, he attacked the forces of Union Major General William S. Rosecrans at Murfreesboro; two battles which ended, at the great cost of 10,000 men, in another stalemate. Convinced that his enemy outnumbered him and exhausted after months of fighting, Bragg lost the will to fight another battle at this time. After a summer of relative inactivity, Bragg fought to regain Chattanooga, which had fallen into Union hands, from a regrouped Rosecrans.

At the resulting Battle of Chickamauga—a two-day fight that resulted in more than 34,000 Confederate and Union losses—Bragg once again gained the upper hand and hoped to crush the whole Union army. He almost succeeded, but allowed the Union to fall back behind fortified Chattanooga. Once again, too, he failed to follow up and consolidate his win by attacking the retreating Federal forces. His failure to follow through at Chickamauga caused most of Davis' generals to urge the Confederate president to relieve Bragg of command. Davis resisted, granting his general another chance to redeem himself.

By late November, however, Bragg was routed out of Tennessee altogether by the stubborn and wily Rosecrans who, unlike his Confederate counterpart, was adored by his troops and trusted by his commanders. On November 25, Bragg's 40,000 troops met with devastating defeat at the battle of Missionary Ridge. Although Bragg's forces had the upper hand in terms of position, morale was low and leadership poor. As the Federal columns moved up, the Confederate center gave way, and what could have been a decisive Confederate victory turned into a rout.

General Bragg, blaming others for his defeat, then resigned his commission in disgust. Davis made him chief of staff, and Bragg was not seen again on the battlefield until 1865, when he commanded a division at the second defense of Wilmington. His lackluster performance there did nothing to reverse the opinion of him held by both his peers and his subordinates. His military career may be said to end here. He died in Galveston, Texas, on September 27, 1876.

Breckinridge, John Cabell
1821–1875

Joining the Confederacy while his home state of Kentucky remained in the Union, the former U.S. vice president and 1860 presidential candidate abandoned politics to serve in the Southern army. Breckinridge had had a stellar career as a state legislator and U.S. congressman, quickly emerging as one of the Democratic party's notable figures. Chosen as James Buchanan's running mate in the 1856 election, Breckinridge, at 35, became the youngest vice president in the country's history.

Although he was a proponent of compromise over the increasingly divisive issues straining the nation, he remained popular with those favoring secession from the Union. When the Democrats split in 1860 over the choice of a presidential nominee, Breckinridge was selected in a special convention as the candidate of the party's Southern faction. With Stephen Douglas heading the ticket for the Northern contingent, the election went to Lincoln, while Breckinridge came in second in the electoral college—winning most of the South—and third in the popular vote.

Remaining in public office, however,

Breckinridge began a term in the U.S. Senate in 1861. There, he defended Kentucky's initial position of neutrality in the Civil War, and was accused of secretly being a Confederate. Learning in October that he was about to be expelled from Congress and arrested, Breckinridge headed south and joined the Confederate army. Although his military experience was limited to service during the Mexican War, he was named division commander and placed in charge of the famous Orphan Brigade of fellow Kentucky confederates. Going on to head an army corps, Breckinridge participated in many of the Civil War's major battles, including Shiloh, Chickamauga, and Missionary Ridge, as well as the siege of Vicksburg and the 1864 Shenandoah Valley Campaign. At the

John C. Breckinridge

December 1862–to–January 1863 Battle of Murfreesboro, Breckinridge came into conflict with his commander, Braxton Bragg, nearly threatening the superior officer to a duel when Bragg blamed him for the Confederate army's defeat. Scraping together a force of fewer than 5,000, which included 250 teenage cadets from the Virginia Military Institute, he stopped a Union drive up the Shenandoah Valley on May 15, 1864, in the Battle of New Market, certainly his most notable military victory.

Jefferson Davis named Breckinridge secretary of war in 1865. Running the department in the Confederacy's waning days, he supervised the evacuation of Richmond before its fall to Grant's army and served as an advisor to Joseph E. Johnston during the Southern general's April surrender negotiations with William Tecumseh Sherman. Breckinridge then fled to Cuba, and lived in Europe and Canada before returning to Kentucky in 1869 to practice law.

Burnside, Ambrose Everett
1824–1881

Insisting that he was unfit for the position, the modest, congenial Union general quickly proved himself correct when he was appointed commander of the Army of the Potomac in late 1862.

Burnside, so renowned for his muttonchop whiskers that the term "sideburns" was coined from his name, served in the Southwest after graduating from West Point. Resigning from the army in 1853 to go into business manufacturing the innovative breech-loading rifle he invented, he went bankrupt and lost his patent, although the "Burnside carbine" became one of the most widely used small arms of the Civil War. He reentered the military in 1861, raising a brigade that performed capably in the First Battle of Bull Run. The following winter, Burnside led an 80-ship, 13,000-troop offensive force in the sounds of North Carolina, battling gale-force storms as well as the Confederate army and navy to capture such vital Southern coastal positions as Roanoke Island, New Berne, Fort Macon, and Beaufort. Promoted to major general, he twice refused offers to take over the Army of the Potomac from his friend George McClellan.

Despite a hesitant performance in the Battle of Antietam, where Burnside's delayed attack on the Confederate right blew the Union's chances for a more conclusive victory, Abraham Lincoln gave him the position in November 1862. The reluctant general accepted on the urging of colleagues who feared that the distrusted and disliked Joseph Hooker would be appointed otherwise. Knowing well that McClellan was fired for failing to take the offensive, Burnside quickly proceeded with plans for an advance on Richmond. That led to one of the North's worst defeats the following month in the Battle of Fredericksburg, where a series of foolhardy frontal assaults did not even come close to dislodging Robert E. Lee's Army of Northern Virginia from its impregnable defenses in the hills behind the town.

Burnside's request to resign in the wake of his demoralizing loss was initially declined, but after his equally ill-considered attempt to get around Lee's forces—the embarrassing "Mud March"—literally bogged down, he was relieved in January 1863, a mere three months after he took command. Reassigned to head the Department of the Ohio, he caused a huge civil liberties controversy by ordering a crackdown on Southern sympathizers, including the arrest of the prominent Copperhead politician Clement Vallandigham for making an antiwar speech. Burnside won acclaim, however, for capturing the notorious Confederate raider, John Hunt Morgan, and for occupying Knoxville in September 1863, and he solidified the Union's control of eastern Tennessee further when he held off a poorly mounted Southern attempt to retake the city.

His performance was far less impressive when he returned to Virginia in 1864 as a corps commander, capped by his spectacular failure to break the Siege of Petersburg in the Battle of the Crater. Sent on an extended leave after the botched attempt to blast through the Confederate line with a huge mine explosion, he was never recalled to duty. After the war, Burnside returned to business, served three terms as governor of Rhode Island before being elected to the U.S. Senate, and became the first president of the National Rifle Association.

Butler, Benjamin Franklin
1818–1893

L oathed in the South and controversial in the North, the near-sighted Union general had the political power to continue receiving important appointments throughout the Civil War, despite a string of battlefield losses and contentious policies.

Butler, a successful Boston criminal attorney, was a prominent Democrat and a staunch supporter of the North's war effort, though he had favored Jefferson Davis for the 1860 presidential nomination. Using his influence to win a military appointment, he achieved an early success in April 1861 quelling pro-secession riots in Baltimore and breaking a blockade on Washington.

The following month, in command at Fortress Monroe, Virginia, Butler earned the South's lasting enmity by declaring that fugitive slaves were a "contraband of war" to be emancipated and employed by the Federal army—and then pressing the Union government to adopt that position officially. In July, he suffered a humiliating loss at Big Bethel in one of the war's first engagements, botching his attempt to advance toward Richmond, but did win a victory two months later at Hatteras Inlet, North Carolina. Leading the ground forces in David Farragut's spring 1862 assault on New Orleans, Butler was named military governor when the city fell.

Although he instituted some civic improvements, Butler's tenure was more noted for his offenses against the populace. Ordering the confiscation of Confederate property, he was accused of filching silverware from homes and churches and acquired the derisive nickname "Spoons." Southerners also called him "Beast Butler" after he issued his infamous "Woman Order," dictating that any woman who insulted a Union soldier be treated like a common prostitute. By December

1862, as corruption and bribery by Northern speculators flourished in his domain, Butler was recalled. He returned to field command back in Virginia late the following year.

In spring 1864, Ulysses Grant gave Butler a chance at glory by ordering him to cut the vital railroad lines between Richmond and Petersburg and attack the Confederate capital. Instead, his force was easily bottled up in May on the tiny Bermuda Hundred peninsula. Butler's mishaps continued as he served under Grant during the Siege of Petersburg, and he was dispatched to New York City in November to prevent election-day rioting by Copperheads. Eager to prove he could do more than quash civilian unrest, Butler obtained command of the land forces in the December 1864

General Benjamin Franklin Butler

attempt to capture Fort Fisher in Wilmington, North Carolina, one of the Confederacy's last open ports. But he called off his ground assault midway, a fiasco that gave Grant an eagerly awaited excuse to relieve him. Butler went back into politics after the war and was elected to Congress in 1866.

By this time a Radical Republican, he became a leader in the efforts to impeach Andrew Johnson and to impose a harsh Reconstruction policy on the South. Butler later served as governor of Massachusetts and, changing political affiliations yet again, ran for president on the Greenback party ticket in 1884.

Chamberlain, Joshua Lawrence
1828–1914

Fighting in many of the Civil War's major battles, the Maine college professor quite possibly saved the Union army from defeat at Gettysburg with his legendary defense of Little Round Top. Chamberlain, a former minister, taught rhetoric, oratory, and modern languages at Bowdoin College. When he was denied a leave of absence to enlist in the military, he took a sabbatical in 1862, ostensibly to perform research in Europe, then headed instead to the army recruiter's office. Appointed lieutenant colonel of the 20th Maine, Chamberlain had been offered a higher rank, which he rejected, asking to "start a little lower and learn the business first." He learned the business quickly enough, serving at Antietam, Fredericksburg, where he was wounded, and Chancellorsville, where he was wounded again.

At Gettysburg on July 2, 1863, the battle's second day, Chamberlain and his 350-man regiment—mostly lumberjacks, trappers, and seamen—was immersed in desperate, fierce fighting to protect the Union's left line. After three previous units had tried and failed, Chamberlain's regiment was ordered to ascend Little Round Top—a rocky, wooded hill critical to the protection of the army's flank—and hold it "at all hazards." An Alabama regiment under Colonel William C. Oakes was poised for attack before Chamberlain's men had finished scrambling up the southern slope. Over a ferocious two-hour period, the Union soldiers managed to beat back a total of five assaults that at times turned into virtual hand-to-hand combat.

But having lost a third of their men and exhausted their ammunition, their situation was desperate as the Confederates readied for another attack. Rather than retreat, however, Chamberlain, remaining remarkably calm under the circumstances, opted for a final, gallant effort to hold the hill. Ordering his men to fix bayonets, he led a sudden charge down the slope that caught the Confederate troops by complete surprise. Dozens surrendered before they even realized that the enemy was unable to return fire, others turned and ran, and Little Round Top, against all odds, remained in Union hands. Wounded a third time during the day's fighting, Chamberlain would later receive the Medal of Honor. Twelve days after he returned to combat duty in May 1864, following a months-long bout with malaria,

Chamberlain was wounded yet again at Petersburg, this time so severely that he was expected to die.

An impressed Ulysses Grant, thinking there was little time left, promoted him brigadier general right on the field. But that wound would not kill Chamberlain for another fifty years; he was not even out of the war. Reaching the rank of major general, Chamberlain was named to accept the Army of Northern Virginia's formal surrender at Appomattox on April 12, 1865.

He declined to remain in the military after the war and returned to Maine. Serving four terms as the state's governor, Chamberlain then became the president of Bowdoin College before dying of his old wartime injury well into the twentieth century.

Crittenden, George Bibb
1812–1880

Crittenden, Thomas Leonidas
1819–1893

The abstract concept of the Civil War as one that set "brother against brother" was realized in a very concrete way in the prominent Crittenden family of Kentucky. A father who had toiled for decades to prevent the Civil War watched his two sons take up arms on opposite sides, one as a Union general, the other as a Confederate. John Jordan Crittenden devoted his life to public service in Kentucky and on the national stage, serving in a variety of positions, including U.S. district attorney, U.S. attorney general (under William H. Harrison, from March to September 1841 and again under Millard Fillmore, from July 1850 to March 1853), and governor of Kentucky (1848 to 1850). Apart from these positions, Crittenden spent the majority of his political life in the U.S. Senate, where he was a forceful voice against secession and where he worked tirelessly to forge a compromise that would save the Union from civil war.

As a Democrat, he opposed the Kansas-Nebraska Act of 1854 because it repealed the Missouri Compromise of 1820 and allowed the prospect of slavery to extend below previously set boundaries, a state of affairs he felt sure would collapse the Union. When Abraham Lincoln was elected president in 1860, Crittenden became the center of the compromise movement in the Senate.

In December 1860, he placed before his congressional colleagues a set of proposals known as the Crittenden Compromise, which attempted to satisfy both sides of the slavery question. When his bill failed to pass and with the country that much closer to war, Crittenden returned home to try to prevent Kentucky from seceding. In that, at least, he was successful, and for the next several months he worked to convince those states that had seceded to reconsider their positions. Crittenden was not an abolitionist, by any means; his fight was not against slavery, but rather for union. To that end, he supported the North until its aims became more involved in the moral issue of slavery itself. Increasingly discouraged, the elderly statesman—he was 74 years old when the war began—watched his two sons fight in a war he had worked so hard to avoid.

His younger son, Thomas Leonidas, followed most closely in his footsteps, becoming a lawyer and serving as a state attorney in the early 1840s. After fighting in the Mexican War, Thomas returned to Kentucky to practice law. Like his father, he was a firm defender of the Union and joined the Northern army at the start of the war. Serving with distinction at Shiloh, Murfreesboro, and in the Tullahoma Campaign, his career was blighted by his actions at Chickamauga, when he was removed from command after his corps was overrun.

Although he was acquitted of all charges, he was demoted and transferred to the Army of the Potomac; he resigned from the army in December 1864. Thomas' older brother, George Bibb, had an altogether different Civil War experience. Unlike his father and brother, George's staunch proslavery views compelled him to join the Confederacy after graduating from West Point and serving in the Mexican War. Made a major general by Jefferson Davis, George accepted an assignment to lead an invasion of his home state of Kentucky. He fought just one major battle, at Mill Springs, and lost badly when his forces were outflanked by Union Brigadier General George H. Thomas. Accused of being drunk during the attack, George was almost courtmartialed then and there, but remained in the army for another several months, serving under Albert Sidney Johnston to regain Tennessee.

His military career survived just another few months, until he was found drunk and his

Thomas L. Crittenden

corps in disarray on April 1, 1862. After being arrested, courtmartialed, and resigning his command, George served out the remainder of the war in various subordinate positions in western Virginia.

Custer, George Armstrong
1839–1876

Custer's 1876 last stand at the Little Bighorn was a suitably flashy end to a military career that began so promisingly during the Civil War. His student days were far from illustrious;

Custer (right), with a Confederate prisoner and former West Point classmate.

Custer graduated last in his 1861 class at West Point. In less than a week he was on the battlefield—and in his element—at First Bull Run, and went on to participate as a cavalry officer in all but one of the major engagements fought by the Army of the Potomac. Custer's audacious and fearless charges—some called them reckless—along with his long, curly golden hair and flamboyant dress, gained him notice quickly.

By June 1863, Custer, only 23, became the Union army's youngest general. Soon after, "the Boy General" distinguished himself on the second day of battle at Gettysburg with a series of headlong attacks that held back Jeb

Stuart's advance on Culp's Hill. Custer faced Stuart again in May 1864 at the Battle of Yellow Tavern, leading his brigade in the charge that killed the Confederate general.

The following month, Custer and his men were responsible for the hardest fighting at Trevilian Station, the war's bloodiest cavalry engagement. But the golden-haired officer's most notable Civil War contribution was in besting Jubal Early's forces in such battles as Winchester and Cedar's Creek during the 1864 Shenandoah Valley campaign. These feats made Custer, who relished fame and glory, a national hero, although the Confederate cavalry by that time had already been severely weakened. Not that the wartime action Custer saw was effortless; his brigade suffered more casualties than any other Union cavalry unit, and over the course of the conflict 11 horses were killed underneath him, though Custer himself was wounded only once. His valuable service continued through the end of the war. He captured four trainloads of supplies at Appomattox Station on April 8, 1865, one of the final death blows to Robert E. Lee's Army of Northern Virginia, which surrendered the following day.

Custer was nearby when the meeting between Grant and Lee took place in Wilmer McLean's house, and he later grabbed a parlor table as a souvenir. After a court-martial for an 1867 incident, he was reinstated in the army, beginning his Indian-fighting career, which brought Custer more of the fame and glory he so loved. His reputation has been considerably diminished by the historic reappraisal of the U.S. government's treatment of Native Americans.

age of 17, he began his military career as an infantryman in Sherman's march to the sea. He was transferred to the cavalry and made an aide to his famous brother upon the elder Custer's promotion to brigadier general in late 1863. His tremendous courage and apparent lack of concern for his own safety earned young Custer a great compliment from the older brother he very much admired: General Custer once told a group of friends, "to show you how much I esteem my brother as a soldier, I believe it is he who should be the general, and I the captain."

As an officer in the 6th Michigan Cavalry, Custer captured Confederate battle flags at great personal risk at Five Forks (April 1, 1865), while leading what proved to be a crucial charge. In that charge he was shot at point-blank range in the face by a Confederate color bearer; the pistol ball entered Custer's left cheek and exited just behind the left ear. He survived the wound, however, and went on to a career as a line officer in the 7th U.S. Cavalry; he died at the head of his troop at the Battle of the Little Bighorn in June 1876, and is buried on the battlefield alongside his men.

Custer, Thomas Ward
1845–1876

The younger brother of General George Armstrong Custer, Brevet Colonel Thomas W. Custer has the distinction of being the only person in any branch of the U.S. Army who received two Congressional Medals of Honor during the Civil War.

Enlisting in the Union army at the tender

Early, Jubal Anderson
1816–1894

Hunched with arthritis, unkempt, feisty, abrasive, and sacrilegious, with a stinging wit and a taste for liquor, "Old Jube," as he was affectionately called by his troops, was an unforgettable character and one of the South's favorite and ablest generals.

A member of an aristocratic Virginia family, Early graduated eighteenth in his 1833 West Point class and fought in the Seminole War and Mexican War. He retired from the army and became a lawyer and legislator, attending his state's 1861 secession convention, where he voted for remaining in the Union.

Once the war began and Virginia joined the Confederacy, however, he returned to the military for the South. After an impressive performance at First Bull Run, Early was promoted to brigadier general. He led a brigade in the spring 1862 Peninsula campaign in Virginia, until he was wounded in the shoulder at the Battle of Williamsburg in May. Recovering quickly, Early led a division in such major battles as Antietam, Fredericksburg, Chancellorsville, Gettysburg, and the Wilderness.

Although he was often perilously impetuous in battle, he proved to be a superb commander and was rapidly promoted. As lieutenant general heading a corps of 14,000, he led his most daring attack—a raid on Washington, D.C., in June and July 1864—that was a shocking setback for the Union. Heading up from the Shenandoah Valley, his troops seized or destroyed property throughout the Maryland countryside. Threatening to burn the villages, Early wrested $20,000 in ransom from Hagerstown and $200,000 from Frederick.

Early's corps crushed a small Federal force near the Monocacy River on July 9 and in two days came within five miles of the Union capital. Its fortifications lightly manned, Washington seemed in serious jeopardy. But Early's advance had been stalled at Monocacy, giving a Union corps time to reinforce the capital, and Early withdrew back into the Shenandoah Valley.

Later that month, Early's troops raided even deeper into the North and burned Chambersburg, Pennsylvania, on July 30 when the town refused to turn over $500,000. Sending Philip Sheridan's forces into the Shenandoah Valley, Ulysses Grant ordered the general to pursue Early "to the death."

A subsequent series of defeats in the valley decimated Early's army. After an old-fashioned yet lethally effective saber charge by Union forces at the Battle of Winchester on September 19, Early lost a quarter of his men. Sheridan's army routed the survivors three days later at Fisher's Hill, forcing Early into a 60-mile retreat.

In a final attempt to hold the valley, the Confederate general led a surprise attack at Cedar Creek at dawn on October 19. What first appeared to be a smashing triumph for Early soon turned into one of the Union army's most decisive victories, when Sheridan's men successfully counterattacked, shattering the Confederate forces and driving them from the region. The following March, Early's small remaining army was badly beaten again by Sheridan in Waynesborough, and Early, relieved of command by a reluctant Robert E. Lee, headed to Texas to join the fighting out West.

The war ended before he arrived, however, so Early went to Mexico, then Cuba and Canada, where he wrote his memoirs. Returning to Virginia in 1869, he resumed practicing law and later worked for the Louisiana state lottery. For the rest of his life,

Early defiantly remained an unreconstructed Confederate and became the first president of the Southern Historical Society.

Farragut, David Glasgow
1801–1870

Rear Admiral David G. Farragut

In his early 60s and after an already distinguished career at sea, Farragut became the Union's favorite Civil War naval hero.

If not born to the sea, he was certainly adopted to it, taken in as a young boy by Commodore David Porter, America's leading early nineteenth-century naval commander. Farragut entered the navy at age nine, and saw action in the War of 1812 as a midshipman. After acquiring a formal education, he returned to the navy, sailing in the Mediterranean, West Indies, and South Atlantic, serving in the Mexican War, and becoming a captain in 1855.

Farragut's home was in Norfolk, Virginia, but at the start of the Civil War he hastily moved North as an ardent supporter of the Union. Although his loyalty was questioned at first by some, and his first Civil War assignment was a modest one—serving on a board that issued officer retirements—Farragut was soon given an important command.

In December 1861, he was made head of the Union's West Gulf Blockading Squadron, and ordered to capture New Orleans, the Confederacy's largest city and major port. Farragut's fleet commenced its attack on the forts guarding the city in early April. Six days

of intense shelling, led by Farragut's foster brother David D. Porter, had little effect, so Farragut made a bold nighttime run on April 24 past the forts, with all but four of his boats smashing through barricades the Confederates had erected in the water. Sinking or running ashore most of the defense squadron in a spectacular fight, Farragut continued on to New Orleans itself, which surrendered the next day.

He followed up that critical victory with the capture of other important lower Mississippi River strongholds, including Baton Rouge and Natchez in the summer of 1862 and Port Hudson in July 1863, although he was unable to take Vicksburg, by far the most strategic. Attempting to tighten the blockade on the Gulf Coast, Farragut captured Galveston in October 1862, which Union forces only held for less than three months, as well as other Texas ports.

In 1864, he turned his sights to an even more important Gulf port still open to blockade runners: Mobile, Alabama. Preparing the assault for nearly seven months, Farragut made his attack on the fortresses and gunboats guarding the heavily mined entrance to Mobile Bay on August 5. In the middle of the three-hour fight, Farragut climbed the mast of his flagship, the *Hartford*, to see above the smoke of battle. Tied to the tall pole because he had vertigo, he made a legendary sight that inspired the entire Union fleet, which abruptly halted when one ship, the ironclad *Tecumseh*, struck a mine and exploded. Farragut shouted what would become an immortal phrase, "Damn the torpedoes! Full speed ahead," and led his squadron through the minefield and by the forts, forcing the surrender of the Confederate flotilla and effectively closing the harbor.

It was his biggest triumph; during a hero's welcome in New York City later that month, Farragut received a gift of $50,000 from grateful civilians, and in December he was promoted to vice admiral, a rank created especially for him. After the war, Farragut became the first U.S. naval officer to be named full admiral and, commanding the navy's European Squadron, led a good-will tour of major foreign ports.

★   ★   ★

Forrest, Nathan Bedford
1821–1877

Rising from private to lieutenant general, Forrest became the Confederacy's most feared cavalry commander, and in the estimation of his foe William T. Sherman, "the most remarkable man our Civil War produced on either side."

Forrest was a poorly educated, self-made man from the deep South who made a fortune as a real estate baron, cotton planter, and slave trader. With no military training, he used his own money to raise a cavalry battalion at the start of the war. Forrest's initial combat fame came after the Union capture of Fort Donelson, Tennessee, in February 1862, when he led his entire unit through enemy lines in a daring escape.

Two months later, his cavalry successfully covered the Confederate army's withdrawal following the Battle of Shiloh, despite Forrest's own serious injury. The fearless horseman then embarked on the first of his notorious lightning raids that terrorized Union forces throughout the war. Destroying railroad and telegraph lines and capturing vital garrisons and arms, Forrest stalled a Federal movement toward Chattanooga in July and halted Ulysses Grant's advance on Vicksburg in December.

A tactical genius with a killer instinct and an invaluable asset on the battlefield as well, he became noted for simple pronouncements that concisely summed up arcane military principles, such as his famous statement, "Get there first with the most men." Led by Braxton Bragg, Forrest fought in the New Year's 1863 Battle of

Murfreesboro, but disgusted with his superior's performance at Chickamauga that September, refused to continue serving under him.

Forrest was given an independent command in Mississippi, and soon led the most controversial foray of his military career. During the capture of Union-held Fort Pillow, Tennessee, in April 1864, Forrest's men were accused of slaughtering, with his encouragement, over 200 unarmed troops—primarily black soldiers who had already surrendered.

In June, he followed that ugly episode with one of his greatest victories. Against a force numberng more than twice his own, Forrest delivered a mortifying defeat at Brice's Cross Roads, Mississippi, inflicting over 2,000 casualties and capturing a huge cache of small arms, artillery, and supply wagons in his rout of the Union forces.

Although the battle diverted Forrest from harassing Sherman's army in its advance toward Atlanta, he continued to wreak havoc on the Union general's supply lines, leading Sherman to call for Forrest's death even "if it cost 10,000 lives and breaks the treasury." But Federal forces could not catch the cunning cavalry leader, and he joined John Bell Hood in the Confederate general's desperate late-1864 invasion of Union-occupied eastern Tennessee.

Not much, in fact, could stop Forrest, a rugged man who over the course of the war had 30 horses shot from under him and was himself wounded four times. But unable to halt the Union's sweep through Alabama in the Confederacy's final days, Forrest, to the surprise of some, surrendered magnanimously in May 1865.

After the war, which ruined him financial-

Lieutenant General Nathan B. Forrest

ly, he went into the railroad business. Also joining the nascent Ku Klux Klan, Forrest became, according to most accounts, its first Grand Wizard in 1867 before resigning over the organization's terrorist bent.

Frémont, John Charles
1813–1890

As a Union general, Frémont's major Civil War contribution was more political than military when he focused Union attention on

General John C. Frémont

the role emancipation should play in the North's war policy.

The magnetic and legendary "Pathfinder" became a national hero early in life for his trailblazing exploits in the Far West. A leader in wresting California from Mexico, he served as one of the state's first senators and got rich in the Gold Rush. Frémont's popularity and his antislavery position were equally instrumental in his being chosen the Republican Party's first presidential nominee in 1856, the youngest man yet to run for the office. With Southern states threatening secession if he were elected, Frémont's loss to James Buchanan forestalled disunion for another four years.

In Europe at the outbreak of the Civil War, he purchased a cache of arms in England for the North on his own initiative and returned to America. Abraham Lincoln, mostly for political reasons, appointed him major general in May 1861, placing him in command of the precarious Department of the West. Based in St. Louis, Frémont spent more energy fortifying the city and developing flashy guard units than equipping the troops in the field. His forces suffered several losses, particularly a major defeat at Wilson's Creek that August.

Attempting to gain a political advantage in the absence of a military one, Frémont, in an unprecedented and unauthorized move, issued a startling proclamation at the end of the month declaring martial law in Missouri and ordering that secessionists' property be confiscated and their slaves emancipated. The action was cheered by antislavery Republicans, but Lincoln, concerned that linking abolition to the war effort would destroy Union support throughout the slave-holding border states, asked Frémont at the very least to modify the order.

The Pathfinder refused, sending his wife, the politically influential daughter of former Senate leader Thomas Hart Benton, to Washington to talk to the president. Displeased with Frémont's effrontery, Lincoln revoked the proclamation altogether and removed him from command. Pressure from his fellow Republicans forced Lincoln to give the popular Frémont another appointment, and in March 1862 he was named head of the army's new Mountain Department, serving in Western Virginia.

Over the following two months, he

endured several crushing losses against Thomas "Stonewall" Jackson during the Confederate general's brilliantly successful Shenandoah Valley Campaign. After a military reorganization placed him under the command of former subordinate John Pope, Frémont angrily resigned his post, never to receive a new Civil War appointment.

In 1864, however, he began another presidential bid with the backing of a cadre of Radical Republicans, but withdrew from the race in September and threw his support to Lincoln after a rapprochement in the party. When he lost most of his fortune by the end of the war, Frémont tried the railroad industry. His reputation damaged by an 1873 conviction for his role in a swindle, he nevertheless resumed his political career, and later in the decade began serving as territorial governor of Arizona.

Grant, Ulysses Simpson
1822–1885

As a Civil War commander, Grant ranked second to none, winning the first major Union victories, earning promotion to general-in-chief of the Union army, and finally receiving General Robert E. Lee's Surrender at Appomattox Court House shortly after his own brilliant months-long Siege of Petersburg had broken the enemy.

That Grant became a true military hero—a cunning strategist with courage, tenacity, and the ability to lead—may have come as a surprise to those who knew him as a young man; indeed, it may have surprised Grant himself. The son of a hardworking, ambitious tanner, Grant was baptized Hiram Ulysses Grant and grew up in the small town of Georgetown, Ohio. A mediocre, rather lazy student, his only love was of horses; he became an accomplished rider at a young age. Despite his poor grades, Grant's father managed to secure him an appointment to West Point through his local congressman, who mistakenly referred to his young constituent as "Ulysses Simpson Grant" in his recommendation to the academy. The name stuck.

Grant's West Point record was far from spectacular. He graduated twenty-first in his class of 39 cadets and was commissioned brevet second lieutenant. Stationed at Jefferson Barracks, near St. Louis, Missouri, he not only began to learn the art of soldiering, but also met the woman who would become his wife, Julia Dent.

A year later, Grant was sent to the Southwest frontier; he served there until the Mexican War, in which he served under "Old Rough and Ready" Zachary Taylor, whose lack of pretense on the battlefield he would later emulate, and Winfield Scott. Grant took part in the Battles of Palo Alto, Monterey, Molino del Rey, where he was made first lieutenant for bravery, and Chapultepec, where he was brevetted captain.

After the Mexicans surrendered, Grant served in various garrisons across the country. His four years at Sackets Harbor, New York, and Detroit, Michigan, were relatively happy ones, largely because Julia Dent, whom he had married in 1848, kept him company. The years

General Grant with his wife, Julia, and son, Jesse, 1864.

that followed in Fort Vancouver and on the West Coast, however, were among the most miserable in his life. Bored and lonely, Grant for the first time, but not the last, took to drinking whiskey. An argument with his commander caused him to resign his commission on April 11, 1854.

Returning to Missouri, Grant tried for several years to support his family. He moved his family to Galena, Illinois, where he worked in his father's leather shop. Barely able to survive during this period, Grant was, in many ways, saved when the Civil War started because it

gave him both a job and a sense of purpose. After the fall of Fort Sumter, Grant helped organize the first company of Union volunteers in Galena.

In June 1861, Grant became colonel of the 21st Illinois Infantry and helped to whip the green troops into an effective fighting force. On August 7, 1861, President Abraham Lincoln appointed Grant brigadier general of volunteers and sent him to occupy Paducah, Kentucky, at the strategic junction of the Ohio and Tennessee rivers.

After a promising start, Grant's first offensive against the Confederates near Belmont, Missouri, ended when Rebel reinforcements arrived in time to drive Grant's troops back. In February 1862, he had a chance to recoup his lost honor when General Henry W. Halleck, his commanding officer, authorized him to move against Forts Henry and Donelson. With 17,000 men and a flotilla of gunboats under the command of Andrew Hull Foote, Grant captured both forts in just over two weeks. At the fall of Fort Donelson, his unyielding statement, "No terms except unconditional and immediate surrender can be accepted," earned him the nickname "Unconditional Surrender" Grant.

His next important battle, at Shiloh, Tennessee, was less than a stunning victory for the Union. It appeared that Grant was surprised by General Albert Sidney Johnston's army when it burst through unfortified Union lines and threatened to drive Grant's men back into the river. Grant was able to regain lost ground through a long battle the following day, but rumors of his incompetence raged for months afterward. His tenacity at Shiloh impressed Abraham Lincoln, however, who is quoted as saying, "I can't spare this man—he fights."

After several months occupying an ambiguous position under Henry Halleck, who took pleasure in spreading rumors about Grant's drinking, Grant was made commander of the Department of Tennessee and charged with the taking of Vicksburg. Although the first few months of the campaign went badly when his supply bases were destroyed by Confederate raiders, Grant turned the situation around by early spring. Claiming "there is nothing left to be done but

to go forward to a decisive victory," Grant devised an unexpected, clever plan and executed it brilliantly. He combined an amphibious movement down the Mississippi past Vicksburg with an overland march through the countryside and back across the river to set up camp behind Confederate lines. Although he had cut himself off from any supply lines, he was able to wait out his enemy during the almost three-month siege that followed.

The Confederate capitulation at Vicksburg on July 4, 1863, marked a turning point in the war and in Grant's own career. Promoted to major general, he next saw action in East Tennessee where, with customary perseverance, he managed to raise the siege of Chattanooga. He then consolidated Union control of the region with victories at Lookout Mountain and Missionary Ridge. Grant's stunning maneuvers brought him both public accolades and professional rewards.

In March 1864, Lincoln promoted him to general-in-chief commanding all the armies of the United States. Grant prepared to launch a coordinated offensive against the Confederacy that spring. For the first time, the four Union armies would work together to hit the Confederates hard enough to force a surrender. Grant planned to maneuver around the Confederate armies and destroy their supply lines behind them. Unfortunately, his well-planned venture became a costly campaign of attrition. The terrible losses of Union as well as Confederate troops earned Grant the ignominious nickname of "Grant the Butcher" in the Northern press.

Lee's army took relentless pounding at the Battles of the Wilderness, Spotsylvania, and

Cold Harbor, but remained strong enough to fight on. In June 1864, Grant and Lee faced each other at Richmond. When Grant failed to make headway there, he adroitly withdrew, crossed the James River, and headed for Petersburg, where he settled down for a siege. For more than nine months the Army of the Potomac worked at cutting Lee's transportation lines and performing indirect assaults on his flanks. In the meantime, Major General William T. Sherman slashed through Georgia and Philip H. Sheridan devastated the Shenandoah Valley.

In April, 1865, the Confederate cause was lost forever when Grant's maneuvers finally stretched the Confederate line to the breaking point. Lee abandoned Richmond and Petersburg on April 2. Marching west, he hoped to join the army of General Joseph E. Johnston and make a final stand. Grant cut him off with a series of battles that finally convinced his worthy opposing general to capitulate. On April 9, 1865, at Appomattox Court House, Virginia, Grant offered Lee generous terms of surrender, which Lee immediately accepted.

After the war, Grant was given the grade of full general in 1866. For a time, he supported President Andrew Johnson's administration, serving as secretary of war after Edwin M. Stanton resigned. Disillusioned with Democrats, he slowly drifted into the Radical Republican camp. With his spectacular war record, he became the natural Republican candidate for president in 1868, an election he won easily.

As president, however, Grant displayed the lack of leadership and discipline his critics had accused him of at the beginning of the war. Although not personally corrupt, his two-term administration became notorious for its scandals and laissez-faire attitude at a time when the country faced an economic depression and struggled with Reconstruction. Grant left office in 1877.

Never an adroit businessman, he lived his last years in poverty, forced to sell his war mementoes and write his memoirs in order to support his family. His *Personal Memoirs* eventually earned the Grant family almost a half million dollars, but Grant died of throat cancer before reaping the book's rewards. He is buried in the mausoleum dedicated to him in 1897 in New York City.

Halleck, Henry Wagner
1815–1872

Known somewhat irreverently as "Old Brains," this Civil War general who served as Abraham Lincoln's general-in-chief for two years was perhaps far more suited to the classroom than the battlefield. His hesitance to send troops to battle, along with his ponderous and scolding nature, ultimately made him an ineffective military leader. His tendency to spread malicious gossip to further his own career—he wrote to Lincoln of rumors about Ulysses S. Grant's drinking—made him one of the most disliked men in Washington.

Born in Westerville, New York, Halleck was educated at the Hudson Academy and studied at Union College before he entered the Military

Academy at West Point. Standing third in a class of 31, Halleck's skills as a military administrator were clear from the start. Immediately after graduation, he was appointed second lieutenant in an engineer corps, a position in which his attention to detail was rewarded with a promotion to the rank of first lieutenant.

During his first years of service, Halleck issued several reports and lectures on military strategy, including a volume entitled *Elements of Military Art and Science,* which gained him a reputation as a skilled and proficient soldier before he ever fought on a battlefield. Sent to the Pacific Coast during the Mexican War, Halleck did not have a chance to prove his fighting mettle there, either. Instead, he spent his time preparing a translation of Baron Antoine Henry Jomini's *Vie politique et militaire de Napoleon,* assisting in the fortification of Monterey, and acting as lieutenant governor of Mazatlan after its capture. He served in several military and civil posts, earning promotion to captain, until he retired from the army in August 1854.

Until the Civil War began, Halleck practiced law in San Francisco and continued his writing career, publishing several books on legal subjects concerning another of his interests: mining. Elected director general of the New Almaden Quicksilver mine and president of the Pacific & Atlantic Railroad, Halleck again displayed remarkable administrative abilities.

At the opening of the Civil War, President Abraham Lincoln appointed Halleck major general in charge of the newly formed Military Department of the Missouri. When Halleck took control, the department was in a state of relative chaos, populated by largely untrained and undisciplined soldiers and with little administrative organization—a state of affairs this gruff man with a love of bureaucracy was imminently willing and able to remedy. In February 1862, Halleck helped set in motion the armies under his command, including those led by Ulysses S. Grant, a man for whom he had little respect but who clearly had more to do with the Union successes that followed than his superior.

Within three months, the Northern forces had chalked up several impressive victories in the West, including the capture of Forts Henry and Donelson and the possession of Nashville, forcing the Confederate Army out of most of Tennessee and Arkansas. After these successes, the Departments of Kansas and Ohio were also placed under Halleck's command, which was now called the Department of the Mississippi. In April 1862, Halleck launched the Shiloh campaign, an ultimately successful but costly Union offensive. After three days of bloody battle, Grant was able to push Confederate General P. T. G. Beauregard's severely depleted and exhausted forces back to Corinth, Mississippi.

It was left to Halleck, who took command of Union forces after Shiloh, to crush Beauregard's army once and for all. With more than three times the army of his enemy, Halleck nevertheless acted with such extreme caution that it took his army more than a month to advance the 20 miles from Shiloh to Corinth, allowing Beauregard—who recognized the futility of mounting a defense—to retreat with what remained of his army. On June 11, Halleck continued to show a remarkable hesitancy in the face of almost certain victory by ordering a halt to the Federal pursuit.

Despite Halleck's lack of aggressiveness, Lincoln appointed him general-in-chief of all the armies of the North. Again, his administrative capabilities impressed even his detractors, but his grasp of field affairs was so poor that his generals often ignored his orders or did their best to circumvent his authority, as Grant did at Vicksburg. In March 1864, Lincoln named Grant supreme commander of all Union armies, thus demoting Halleck by sending him upstairs to the new post of chief of staff, where he remained until the end of the war. After the war, he continued to serve in the military, first in the Pacific and then in Kentucky until his death in 1872.

Hampton, Wade
1818–1902

With no formal military education, one of the South's richest planters rose to become commander of the Confederate cavalry after the death of Jeb Stuart.

Hampton's experience running his family's vast South Carolina cotton plantations led him to doubt the economic wisdom of slavery, though he did not oppose the institution in principle. Also skeptical about secession, Hampton nevertheless used his own money at the outbreak of the Civil War to raise a unit of infantry, cavalry, and artillery for the Confederate army.

As its colonel, he led his unit, known as "Hampton's Legion," into battle at First Bull Run in July 1861, where he was slightly wounded. Participating in the Peninsula campaign of spring 1862, Hampton was wounded again at the Battle of Seven Pines. After recovering, he was assigned to the Army of Northern Virginia's cavalry as a brigadier general. Hampton fought at Antietam and, as second-in-command, joined Jeb Stuart in his celebrated October ride around George McClellan's army in Maryland.

Wounded a third time at Gettysburg, the legendarily robust and athletic Hampton returned to duty later in 1863. With the new rank of major general, he led a cavalry division in the Battle of the Wilderness in May 1864. Although Hampton was the ranking officer, he was not immediately appointed Jeb Stuart's successor when the commander of Robert E. Lee's cavalry corps was killed four days later at Yellow Tavern. Hampton was ultimately given the position in August and, the following month, proved his merit in a daring raid that nabbed nearly 2,500 head of cattle for ravenous Confederate troops entrenched at Petersburg.

When the South started suffering a shortage of horses as well as food, he began training his cavalry to fight on foot. In January 1865, Hampton returned to South Carolina, where he tried to raise military equipment and civilian morale. There, he also commanded Joseph E. Johnston's cavalry corps during the Confederate general's struggle against the invading Union army of William Tecumseh Sherman. Hampton avoided surrendering with Johnston in April and considered making a final stand for the Confederacy in the West. Instead, he returned to his home and worked to rebuild his ravaged plantations.

After the Reconstruction era, Hampton

became a major force in South Carolina politics for a generation, serving as both governor and U.S. senator.

Hancock, Winfield Scott
1824–1886

"My politics are of a practical kind—the integrity of the country, the supremacy of the Federal government, an honorable peace or none at all." This clever, tenacious general who fought in many of the war's major battles, including Gettysburg, earned the admiration of his troops and the respect of his commanders. His integrity, lack of political ambition, and his concentration on the matter at hand—namely the discipline and training of his men—made him one of the Union's most valuable soldiers.

Born in Pennsylvania, Hancock graduated from West Point in 1844. Breveted second lieutenant, he served first at Fort Towson on the frontier before being stationed in Mexico as that country headed toward war. In the Mexican War, under the command of General Winfield Scott, Hancock fought in four principal battles for which he was awarded a brevet to first lieutenant. Between the Mexican War and the Civil War, Hancock continued to improve his skills as a soldier against the Seminoles in Florida (1855), in Kansas under General Harney (1857–58), and during the Mormon uprising in Utah (1859).

Fort Sumter fell while Hancock was serving as chief quartermaster of the Southern District of California; he immediately requested a transfer to active duty in the East. He was then appointed brigadier general of volunteers and assisted in organizing the Army of the Potomac. Under General George B. McClellan, he played an important role in the Battles of Williamsburg and Frazier's Farm during the Peninsula campaign, at Antietam where he commanded the first division of the 2nd Army Corps, and during the Battle of Fredericksburg.

After the Battle of Chancellorsville, as Union forces attempted to stop Robert E. Lee's invasion of the North at Pennsylvania, President Lincoln appointed Hancock commander of the entire 2nd Army Corps. At the same time, Lincoln made another change in command by replacing General Joseph Hooker with General George Gordon Meade just as the Confederate army faced its foe in the tiny town of Gettysburg, Pennsylvania.

Hancock helped Meade to choose an excellent position for the Union army on the first day of battle. On the second day, his army was able to push back Lee's attack on the Union left flank. Riding up and down the front lines of battle to inspire and command his men, Hancock was heard to say, "There are times when a corps commander's life does not count." Indeed, Hancock received serious wounds at Gettysburg from which he never fully recovered.

Nevertheless, after recuperating for only six months, Hancock returned to his corps and fought through the Virginia campaigns of 1864. In the Battle of the Wilderness, Hancock pulled off a major reversal after his corps was nearly crushed by a flank maneuver led by

General Winfield S. Hancock (seated).

James Longstreet. Instead of retreating, Hancock ordered his men to form a new line of battle across a north-south road along which the Confederates were advancing; when the Confederates arrived, they were stopped and driven back.

Hancock showed the same courage and tenacity at Spotsylvania, Cold Harbor, and at Petersburg; in recognition for his service in these battles, he was appointed brigadier general in the Regular army on August 12, 1864. Later that month, the man so devoted to his troops was disheartened and saddened when a surprise Confederate attack at Reams Station during the Petersburg campaign devastated his corps.

Shortly after this defeat, Hancock, exhausted after three long years in battle, was reassigned to Washington, D.C. to recruit a corps of veterans. He remained in the capital, except for a brief term as commander of the Middle Military Division of Virginia, until the end of the war.

His career as a soldier was far from over, however. In July 1866, Hancock became major general in the Regular army and fought in the Missouri Indian wars. He then went on to assume a post in the South as part of the North's Reconstruction effort as commander of the 5th Military District covering Texas and Louisiana. Hancock found the military's role in Reconstruction offensive, and angered many Radical Republicans by refusing to carry out certain measures, including replacing civil courts with military ones. He asked for and was granted a transfer to the North, eventually assuming command of the Department of the East.

By this time, Hancock's reputation as an honest, intelligent leader—as well as a bona fide war hero and anti-Reconstructionist—prompted the Democrats to nominate him for president in 1880. He lost to Republican James Garfield, another war veteran, by a small margin of the popular vote.

On August 8, 1885, Hancock carried out his last official public duty of national importance, which was conducting General Ulysses S. Grant's funeral. This was an appropriate gesture since Grant held his corps commander in the highest esteem, once remarking that "[Hancock's] genial disposition made him friends, and his personal courage and his presence with his command in the thickest of the fight won him the confidence of troops serving under him." Hancock died on Governor's Island, New York, on February 9, 1886.

Hardee, William Joseph
1815–1873

Lieutenant General William J. Hardee, grandson of a Revolutionary War veteran and son of a cavalry major in the War of 1812, was born to military tradition and served it well. Born in Camden County, Georgia, Hardee attended the U.S. Military Academy at West Point and graduated with the class of 1838.

Assigned to the Second Dragoons, a regiment of note, Hardee quickly rose to first lieutenant and later to captain. He was sent to Europe with a military commission to study the operations of continental cavalry regiments, and upon his return was assigned to duty as a tactical officer in Louisiana, at Fort Jesup.

Twice brevetted for gallantry in the Mexican War, Hardee was involved in the seige of Vera Cruz, the Battles of Contreras and Molino del Rey, and the taking of Mexico City. As a result of both his travels in Europe and his experiences in Mexico, Hardee undertook the writing of what he is perhaps best known for: *Rifle and Light Infantry Tactics*, popularly known as "Hardee's Tactics," published in 1855—just in time to become a premier manual of instruction to both the United States and Confederate States Armies.

Hardee was senior major of the famous 2nd U.S. Cavalry, which boasted among its officer corps Colonel Albert Sidney Johnston, Lieutenant Colonel Robert E. Lee, and Junior Major George H. Thomas, Jr. Later assigned to a position of commandant of cadets at West Point, Hardee was on leave in his home state when Georgia's legislature voted for secession on January 19, 1861. Sources disagree on the date of Hardee's resignation from the U.S. Army; some say as early as January 21, others date it 10 days later. However, by June 17, Hardee was a brigadier general in the Confederate army, and a major general before the end of 1861.

Hardee's first assignment involved the organizing of a brigade of troops from Arkansas, which later was dubbed "Hardee's Brigade" in the general's honor. Transferred in the fall of 1861 to Kentucky, Hardee participated throughout the war in some of the hardest-fought battles of the Western Confederate army, known as the Army of Tennessee. Hardee was at Shiloh in April 1862, and Perryville, in October of the same year.

Promoted to lieutenant general to rank from October 10, Hardee was commander of the left wing of the army during Braxton Bragg's campaigns in Kentucky, and at Murfreesboro he was responsible in large part for Bragg's strong offensive on the Federal right at dawn on December 31, 1862.

In July 1863, Hardee was replaced by D. H. Hill as commander of Bragg's 2nd Corps and ordered to Mississippi, only to be similarly caught up in a government-ordered shakeup of the command structure when he was replaced by General Leonidas K. Polk. Hardee later commanded a corps at Chattanooga and shortly thereafter refused command of the Army of Tennessee, and after the fall of Atlanta in 1864, received command of the military departments of South Carolina, Georgia, and Florida.

He assisted General Joseph E. Johnston in the campaign to contain Union General Sherman's March to the Sea, but found he had insufficient men or supplies to do anything more than harrass and annoy Sherman's seemingly unstoppable progress through the heart of the Confederacy. On December 18, 1864, Hardee was forced to evacuate Savannah and withdrew into South Carolina after refusing Sherman's suggestion that he surrender his army.

A month later Sherman came forth from Savannah and pursued Hardee, who was unable to defend Charleston and had to finally retreat further into North Carolina, meeting up eventually with Joseph Johnston once more. Before anything much could be made of a joint effort between them, Hardee received word of the surrender of Robert E. Lee's army at Appomattox; it was not long after that before Johnston also realized the futility of continuing the fight and surrendered at Durham Station, North Carolina, on April 26, 1865.

Hardee retired to a plantation near Selma, Alabama, after the war, having married in 1863 at the height of his fame. He died while on a trip to Wytheville, Virginia, in 1873, and is buried in Selma. His was a distinguished career of military service, which led even opponents and former comrades such as Sherman and Thomas to refer to him as a competent and capable soldier. From his own people he received even more accolades, being described by E. A. Pollard as a man possessed of a "courage . . . of an order which inspires courage in others."

Hill, A(mbrose) P(owell)
1825–1865

Hill was one of Robert E. Lee's favorite lieutenants, but his best Civil War service actually came before he was promoted to high command. From a prominent Virginia family,

Hill attended West Point, where his roommate was future Union commander George McClellan. His courtship of McClellan's fiancée went awry when the woman heard rumors that Hill had gonorrhea, an illness that may explain Hill's frequent sick leaves late in the Civil War. Said to be an opponent of slavery, he still resigned from the Federal army to serve with the Confederacy even before his state seceded.

Hill proved audacious, if impetuous, in battle, gaining early notoriety as the leader of "Hill's Light Division." Celebrated for its nimble and unencumbered advances, the unit performed magnificently in the Peninsula campaign of spring 1862 despite heavy losses. Many of these came in the Seven Days campaign, when Hill, lacking the expected support from Stonewall Jackson, nevertheless led an assault against the solidly entrenched Union line at Mechanicsville on June 26. He and his men were left largely to their own devices again the following day at Gaines' Mill, and again later in the week at White Oak Swamp. Hill and Jackson's efforts would be better coordinated over the next year in such victories as Second Bull Run, Cedar Mountain, Fredericksburg, and Chancellorsville.

Although they made a splendid team, the two men clashed occasionally, with Jackson even arresting Hill for insubordination shortly before the Battle of Antietam. His punishment suspended by Lee for the campaign, Hill's timely arrival on the field—in his characteristic red battle shirt—knocked the attacking Union left flank back across Antietam Creek and saved the Confederate army from a catastrophic defeat. When Jackson was shot at Chancellorsville, Hill temporarily took his command until he was wounded himself, then was promoted to lieutenant general by Lee following Jackson's death. A month later, one of Hill's divisions kicked off the Battle of Gettysburg as it approached the Pennsylvania town in search of a desperately needed supply of shoes. In a lackluster performance, Hill also commanded a corps in the May 1864 Battle of the Wilderness, but illness kept him from several of the Army of Northern Virginia's later engagements. He was on hand, however, during the Union's final assault on Petersburg in April 1865. Rallying his troops on April 2, Hill was shot through the heart, his death yet another devastating blow for Lee.

Hill, Daniel Harvey
1821–1889

Born in York District, South Carolina, Daniel H. Hill was a member of the West Point class of 1842 from which a dozen young cadets, including James Longstreet, were destined to gain generals' stars in the War Between the States.

Hill participated in the Mexican War, being in most of the crucial battles of that war, receiving brevet ranks for gallantry at Chapultepec and Churubusco. At the close of the conflict he resigned his commission and turned to teaching mathematics at Washington College, Lexington, Virginia (later to become Washington and Lee). He later taught the same subject at Davidson College, and was thus engaged until accepting an appointment as superintendent of the North Carolina Military Institute in 1859.

Hill was responsible for organizing North Carolina's first camp of military instruction upon the secession of his state in 1861, and in July of that year was appointed brigadier general, one month after commanding the First North Carolina Infantry at the battle of Big Bethel. Less than a year later, Hill was promoted to major general, and saw service in Joseph E. Johnston's command at Williamsburg, Yorktown, and Seven Pines.

Robert E. Lee's reports following the Seven Days campaign give a great deal of praise to Hill's handling of his division, and he is cited for excellent conduct at Second Manassas (Second Bull Run) and South Mountain; during the latter engagement he protected the Confederate supply train by holding off the attacks of a significantly larger Union force with only 5,000 men.

It was widely held for many years that the strayed copy of Lee's famous "Lost Order" had been mislaid by Hill at Sharpsburg (Antietam), a charge which Hill roundly denied in the postwar years. In that same battle, Hill had the dubious distinction of losing a mount in what has to be the most bizarre and embarrassing instance of a horse's death recorded in the tragic annals of war. While engaged in reconnaissance with Robert E. Lee and James Longstreet, both of whom had dismounted lest they draw enemy fire, Hill had no sooner been told he, too, ought to dismount when a Federal shell struck their position, neatly removing the forelegs of Hill's charger. The general was only able to dis-

mount from the animal by clambering over its rump in an ungainly fashion.

Hill was one of those responsible for the protection of Richmond while the Army of Northern Virginia invaded Pennsylvania in July 1863. Shortly after that he was appointed lieutenant general and was transferred to the army of Braxton Bragg in Tennessee. After the Battle of Chickamauga, Hill signed a petition requesting that Bragg be relieved of command for incompetence, a move which did little to ingratiate him to Bragg's chief supporter, President Jefferson Davis. The president refused to ask Congress to confirm Hill's promotion, and relieved him of command of his corps to boot; not until the battle of Bentonville, a three-day inconclusive fight in the closing days of the last stand in the Carolinas, was Hill allowed to command troops in the field.

D. H. Hill was one of the generals who participated in Joseph Johnston's surrender at Durham Station, near Greensboro, North Carolina, on April 26, 1865.

Hill returned to Charlotte, North Carolina, upon his parole, and in 1866 established a popular monthly periodical, *The Land We Love*. Three years later, he also instituted a weekly newspaper called *The Southern Home*. He became deeply interested in education, citing a need to vindicate the "truth of Southern history" and to train young men in agriculture and industrialization. To this end, Hill became president of the University of Arkansas, a post he held until illness required him to take leave of absence in 1884.

In 1886, Hill accepted the presidency of the Middle Georgia Military and Agricultural

College, which later became the Georgia Military College, a position he held until his death. He also did a great deal of writing in view of a desire to set the record straight on the Confederacy's behalf, and was a contributor to many historical collections and publications, including the *Battles and Leaders of the Civil War* series. General Hill died in Charlotte, North Carolina, in 1889, and is buried in the Davidson College Cemetery, Davidson, North Carolina.

General John B. Hood

Hood, John Bell
1831–1879

Lacking neither courage nor fighting skills, Hood's deficient strategic abilities and ill-suitedness to high command helped cause the destruction of the Confederacy's Army of Tennessee late in the war.

The tall and imposing Kentucky native graduated in the bottom fifth of his class at West Point, and his early military service included a stint in the elite 2nd Cavalry, during which he had already begun to demonstrate bold, if reckless, tendencies.

Leaving the U.S. Army in April 1861 to join the Confederacy, he and his famed brigade of Texans made noteworthy showings in the Seven Days battles, Second Bull Run, and Antietam, where they sustained heavy casualties breaking the Union's initial attack. A gunshot wound at Gettysburg crippled Hood's left arm, and he lost his right leg later in 1863 in the Battle of Chickamauga. Thereafter, he

had to be strapped to his horse before each day's fighting, but the injuries did not slow his military advancement.

As Joseph E. Johnston's chief officer in the 1864 defense of Atlanta against William T. Sherman's invading Union army, Hood roundly criticized his superior's cautious strategy. In July, he was given the chance to do better, when Jefferson Davis, eager for a hard fighter, appointed Hood to take over the Army of Tennessee from Johnston in the middle of the campaign. Within two days of gaining command, Hood went on the offensive, playing into Sherman's hands. His three attacks against the Union army—at Peachtree Creek, near Decatur, and at Ezra Church—cost him 15,000 men, and he was forced to retreat back to Atlanta's strong fortifications. The city was besieged and, a month later, fell to the North. Hood still managed an effective withdrawal of his troops and, with help from Nathan Bedford Forrest, attacked the Union's supply lines in north Georgia and Tennessee.

Hardly halting Sherman's relentless "March to the Sea," though, the impetuous Confederate conceived a bolder—and hopelessly unrealistic—plan: an all-out invasion of Tennessee. Along with forcing Sherman to turn and fight, he hoped to retake the state altogether, and then, advancing further northeast and collecting reinforcements, he could even crush Ulysses S. Grant's forces in Virginia from the rear. Instead, Hood's outnumbered men wound up confronting John Schofield's entrenched troops in Franklin. On November 30, against the furious objections of his lieutenants, he ordered a massive assault on the fortified Union line. After over a dozen valiant but futile charges, Hood lost a quarter of his army. Losing the confidence of the survivors as well, he nevertheless proceeded north to Nashville, this time encountering George Henry Thomas.

With his depleted force camped outside the city, Hood ran out of ideas and waited, first for reinforcements that never arrived, then for Thomas' inevitable attack. When it came, an overpowering two-day onslaught in mid-December, the Army of Tennessee virtually disintegrated. Retreating deeper and deeper South with what was left of his force, a despondent Hood resigned his command in January of 1865. After the war, he went into

business in New Orleans, where he, his wife, and one of his eleven children died in a yellow fever epidemic four years later.

Hooker, Joseph
1814–1879

Hooker earned the celebrated nickname he so disliked, "Fighting Joe Hooker," with his aggressive tactics, though he faltered at his most critical juncture, leading the Union army in its devastating defeat at Chancellorsville.

The cocky, once-dashing military man's early service included West Point administrative work, border duty in the Far West, and action in the Seminole War and Mexican War. With a knack for getting on the wrong side of his superiors, he left the army to take up farming in California. Hooker attempted to reenlist at the start of the Civil War but, perhaps because of his troublemaking reputation, was initially denied a commission. After he received his military appointment in May 1861, Hooker directed the defense of Washington, D.C., that summer and distinguished himself in the Peninsula campaign the following spring.

Leading the Union's dawn attack at Antietam in September 1862, he was seriously wounded, but recovered to command a corps in the Battle of Fredericksburg three months later. Hooker freely criticized his commander Ambrose Burnside for the Union's embarrassing loss there, nursing an ambition to head the Army of the Potomac himself. He got his wish

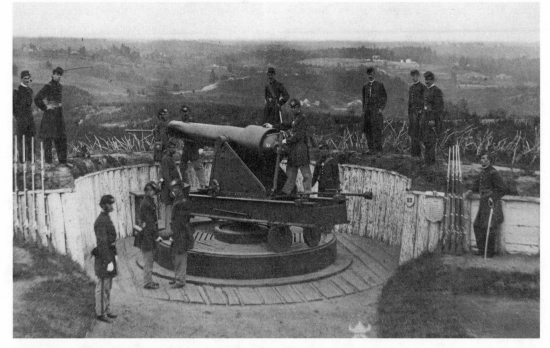

Major General Joseph Hooker led the defense of Washington, D.C., summer 1861.

on January 26, 1863, when Abraham Lincoln appointed him to succeed Burnside, who had only accepted the position originally because he did not want Hooker to have it. The president, somewhat apprehensive about the choice and annoyed at Hooker's comment to a reporter that the Union needed a good dictator, acerbically wrote his new commander, "What I ask of you is military success and I will risk the dictatorship."

A popular choice among the dispirited troops, Hooker began by boosting morale, effectively reorganizing the army and cleaning up the camps. He also cleaned up his own behavior, trying to live down his well-earned reputation as a hard drinker and gambler, whose rowdy headquarters were likened to "a combination of barroom and brothel." (Notwithstanding the widespread belief, the slang term "hooker" predates the general.) Remaining sober and on relatively good behavior, what he could not do was deliver the "military success" that Lincoln requested. Hooker planned a bold assault on Robert E. Lee's Army of Northern Virginia, but lost his nerve in the face of a greatly outnumbered Confederate force at Chancellorsville in early May. Ordering his troops to fall back as the battle commenced, Hooker lost his advantage and, hampered by a concussion from a shell blast, continued to act with uncharacteristic hesitation throughout the engagement. With a humbling defeat that cost him 17,000 men, he was hesitant to confront Lee again, even though the Confederate general was preparing to invade the North. Lincoln removed Hooker from the Army of the Potomac's command on June 28, 1863, three days before the Battle of Gettysburg began.

He was sent west, where he fought with his old resolve at Chattanooga in October, leading the Union's gutsy charge up Lookout Mountain, and during the summer 1864 siege on Atlanta. Miffed when he was not given command of the Army of the Tennessee upon the death of James McPherson, Hooker resigned his post, and spent the rest of the war out of action in the Midwest. He remained with the Regular army until debilitated by a stroke in 1868.

Jackson, Thomas Jonathan "Stonewall"
1824–1863

Remarkable bravery, precise attention to military detail, and the ability to engender loyalty and inspire devoted service from his men combined to make Thomas "Stonewall" Jackson an irreplaceable member of the Confederate army. Known for his deep religious convictions, his exemplary personal habits (he never smoked or drank), and his unrelenting insistence on strict discipline within his ranks, Jackson nevertheless was one of the army's most popular leaders. He also appeared to possess a kind of second sight during battle. Able to disappear from enemy view—sometimes accompanied by more than

15,000 men—he would then turn up just in time to attack his enemy's weakest point.

Orphaned at an early age and brought up by an uncle, Jackson grew up in rural Virginia and barely received even a middle school education. Through sheer will he made it through West Point; ever determined, he managed to graduate in the top third of his 1842 class. Like so many of his Civil War comrades, Jackson first saw action in the Mexican War. Under John B. Magruder, Jackson fought well at Vera Cruz, Contreras, and Chapultepec. After the Mexican War, Jackson served for a time in Florida during the Seminole uprising. He left the army in 1851 to join the faculty of the Virginia Military Institute at Lexington, where he taught philosophy and artillery techniques for almost a decade.

Jackson and a corps of his cadets were present at what some would say was the spark that set the Civil War off: the hanging of John Brown in 1859. Like many of his Confederate compatriots, Jackson would have preferred that the issues dividing the nation be solved with politic compromise that would allow the Union to persist. When his home state of Virginia seceded, however, he felt compelled to defend the South and joined the Confederate army. His first assignment involved bringing a battalion of cadets to Richmond to serve as drillmasters.

In April 1861, Jackson was made a colonel of the infantry and sent to Harpers Ferry. There he organized what would become known as the "Stonewall Brigade," the only brigade to have an officially designated nickname, which it received from the Confederate Congress on May 30, 1863. Composed of five

Virginia regiments from the Shenandoah Valley, the brigade of 4,500 raw recruits underwent weeks of Jackson's grueling training program, which managed to turn them into a quite effective military organization.

Their first chance to prove their mettle came in July, during the Battle of First Bull Run. As commander of a brigade under Albert Sidney Johnston, Jackson ordered his men to bolster the Confederate left flank at a crucial point in the battle. His bravery, and the bravery of his men, earned Jackson the famous nickname; a nearby colleague was so impressed with his stalwart behavior, he remarked, "There is Jackson standing like a stone wall." For his service at Bull Run, he was elevated to major general on October 7, 1861, and was sent to assume command in the Shenandoah Valley.

Jackson's assignment in the valley was, at first, largely a tactical one: to create a diversion that would keep troops under Nathaniel Banks from joining George B. McClellan's forces as they headed toward Richmond. Jackson's total strength was about 10,000 men, while Banks commanded nearly twice that number. Although the first part of his campaign went poorly, Jackson managed to pull off one of the most brilliant maneuvers in military history early in the spring of 1862 during his Shenandoah Valley campaign. For nearly three months, Jackson and his men attacked Union troops where and when they least expected it, defeating three separate Union armies in five battles. With just 17,000 men (reinforcements arrived during the campaign), Jackson played a crucial role in Robert E. Lee's successful attempt to stop McClellan's drive to the Confederate capital.

General Thomas "Stonewall" Jackson, two weeks before his death.

After their coup in the valley, Jackson and his command were transferred to the Richmond area in time to fight in the Seven Days campaign. Perhaps still exhausted and certainly unfamiliar with the terrain, Jackson seemed to lose his otherwise impeccable sense of battle readiness as well as his automatic obedience to his commanding officer—this lapse caused some of his colleagues to question his sanity. At both Mechanicsville and White Oak Swamp, he failed to deliver his troops as Robert E. Lee commanded, putting the entire Army of Northern Virginia in jeopardy.

Jackson managed to recover his skills, perhaps simply by resting, in time to display his more characteristic genius at Second Bull Run.

Jackson and his men undertook a grueling 51-mile march across Virginia to Manassas Junction, a trip they concluded in just two days. Once there, Jackson was able to so thoroughly confuse Union General John Pope as to his whereabouts that the Confederates—once again with less than half the manpower of their opponents—won another victory.

Jackson's unique ability to inspire his troops and to remain prepared to fight was once again on display at Antietam. Lee's plan to invade the North for a second time depended upon the capture of the federal garrison at Harpers Ferry. Jackson accomplished this on September 15, 1862, giving him just enough time to move his troops back to Antietam, possibly saving Lee's army from total destruction. On October 10, 1862, Jackson was promoted to lieutenant general and was given command of the 2nd Corps in the Army of Northern Virginia.

At the battle of Fredericksburg on December 13, he led the right wing of the army to victory. Having fought long and hard, this devoted family man then took time off to visit his wife, who had just given birth to a baby daughter. He was called back almost immediately with the news that almost 135,000 Federal troops were crossing the Rappahannock on both sides of Fredericksburg. Dividing his forces, Jackson headed toward Lee, sending one division to stop Major General John Sedgwick's left flank. Together, Lee and Jackson were able to drive the Federals, led by Hooker, back to Chancellorsville on May 1.

That night, Lee and Jackson devised a remarkable plan: in the face of military logic, they decided to further divide the army. Lee would stay at Chancellorsville to face Hooker's front while Jackson made a sweeping flank movement around Hooker's right to attack from the rear. Jackson's tricky maneuver succeeded and he and his men were able to rout the Federal right flank and win the battle.

Unfortunately, the pinnacle of his military career came during his last few hours of life. In the faint light of dusk, some of Jackson's own men mistakenly fired at their beloved leader. One bullet penetrated the palm of his right hand, a second passed through his left wrist, and a third splintered the bone of his left arm. His injured left arm was amputated, and for a brief time it appeared he would survive. Unfortunately, his condition was complicated by pneumonia, and he died on May 10, 1862.

Johnston, Albert Sidney
1803–1862

Considered the ablest professional soldier to join the Confederacy, this Texas maverick was killed in action just a year after the Civil War began, striking a devastating blow to the Confederate military.

Eighth in the West Point class of 1826, Johnston saw action in several theaters in the 35 years between graduation and the start of the Civil War. His first post took him to the frontier, where he fought in the Black Hawk War. He resigned from the army in 1834 to care for his ailing wife, who died the following year. A true adventurer, Johnston then settled in the republic of Texas in 1836, enlisting as a private in the Texas army. Named senior brigadier general, he later became the republic's secretary of war. Resigning in 1840 to try his hand at farming in Brazoria County, he soon returned to the battlefield during the Mexican War, where he fought under General Zachary Taylor on the Rio Grande.

He continued to climb the ranks of the military as colonel of the 2nd U.S. Cavalry division in 1849 and commander of the Department of Texas in 1856. Breveted to brigadier general in 1857, Johnston was posted in Utah. When the Civil War began, he was living in California as commander of the Department of the Pacific. Although he supported the idea of union and had hoped for a compromise between North and South, Johnston chose to fight for the Confederacy when the Civil War began.

Federal authorities, loathe to lose such a promising soldier, took steps to block his passage back home from California, but with a firm resolve to stand by his adopted home state of Texas, Johnston managed to safely return to the South.

He arrived in Richmond in mid-September and was at once appointed commander of the Confederate Department of the Mississippi, a huge territory stretching from the Appalachian Mountains in the east to the Indian Territories in the west. Although woefully undermanned and undersupplied, Johnston's army made a bold first move by invading Kentucky and establishing a bulkhead there to protect Tennessee from a Union offensive. Constantly urging the Confederate government to reinforce his 4,000 troops, Johnston was able to hold the Union in check until January 1862,

General Albert S. Johnston

when General Ulysses S. Grant attacked Tennessee with full force.

Johnston, realizing that Fort Donelson on the Cumberland River was the linchpin of Confederate control of Tennessee, pulled resources from the indefensible Fort Henry to protect it. Indeed, Fort Henry was Grant's first target upon his ascent of the Tennessee River early in February, and he was able to capture it quickly. Led by Brigadier General John B. Floyd and Major General Gideon J. Pillow, Johnston's troops fought hard at Fort Donelson, but were forced to surrender on February 16.

With Fort Donelson lost, Johnston retreated south from his headquarters in Nashville, writing to his superiors that he was leaving behind a "scene of panic and dismay." Amassing a force of 17,000 men at Murfreesboro, Johnston planned to defend the Mississippi Valley from an anticipated Federal thrust. When forces under P.G.T. Beauregard arrived, Johnston's troops numbered more than 44,000. The extra forces allowed Johnston to take the offensive and surprise the enemy with an attack on Grant's 39,000 men situated on the west bank of the Tennessee River—and to do so before Major General Don Carlos Buell's 36,000 troops converged with Grant's.

On Sunday, April 3, he led his men on what was expected to be a simple one-day march. Unfortunately, heavy rains and unfamiliar territory considerably slowed the advance. Fearing that the two days lost in travel meant that Buell's men had arrived— and some of them had—Beauregard urged Johnston to call off the attack and retreat to Corinth. Johnston replied with typical resolve, "I would fight them if they were a million."

At dawn on April 6, he mounted his horse to lead his men to the gruesome two-day Battle of Shiloh, the first engagement of the Civil War with heavy loss of life, and a devastating defeat for the Confederates. On the first day, as Johnston attempted to regroup his critical east flank in thick woodlands near the Peach Orchard, he was struck in the leg by a minié bullet. He bled to death within minutes.

President Davis, upon hearing of his fallen friend and valued commander, offered a special message to Congress in which he said of Johnston, "In his death he has illustrated the character for which through life he was conspicuous—that of singleness of purpose and devotion to duty with his whole energies."

Johnston, Joseph Eggleston
1807–1891

Though in perpetual conflict with Jefferson Davis, who mistook his defensive fighting strategies for a lack of will, Johnston continued to hold top Confederate commands throughout the Civil War in both the eastern and western theaters.

The compact and fiercely intelligent Virginian, a West Point graduate and civil engineer, had earlier fought and been wounded in the Seminole War and Mexican War, and served in "Bleeding Kansas" during the tense 1850s. Appointed the U.S. Army's quartermaster general in 1860, he resigned the following April to join the Confederacy.

Johnston's initial assignment was in the Shenandoah Valley, from there leading his units to Manassas Junction in July to reinforce Pierre G. T. Beauregard's troops at First Bull Run. Officially in command of the combined forces, he deferred to Beauregard's superior knowledge of the field, and the Southerners routed the Union army in a startling victory.

Johnston was named one of the South's five full generals the following month, launching his first disagreement with Davis when he complained about not receiving the proper seniority. Still placed in charge of the Confederacy's Virginia forces, he faced George McClellan's Army of the Potomac in an uncontested standoff near Washington, then confronted the Union commander at the beginning of the North's spring 1862 advance on Richmond. Johnston wanted to take up the solid defenses outside the Confederate capital, but Davis insisted he hold the invading troops east on the Virginia peninsula. Making a series of canny tactical retreats anyway, Johnston then launched an attack at Seven Pines on May 31. He was seriously wounded in the indecisive battle, and was succeeded by Robert E. Lee.

After a six-month recovery, Johnston was given the unwieldy, ambiguous general command of Confederate armies in the West. In spring 1863, he directed John C. Pemberton, whose troops at Vicksburg were facing Ulysses S. Grant's superior numbers, to evacuate and help him consolidate their separated forces, while Davis issued contrary orders to defend the Mississippi River stronghold at all costs. With Johnston unable to relieve the besieged Confederates, Vicksburg fell to the North on July 4. The commander and the Southern president, seething in mutual dislike, blamed each other for the defeat. But Johnston was revered by his troops and popular with the public, and Davis was compelled to place him in charge of the Army of Tennessee in December 1863.

Opposing William T. Sherman's advance against Atlanta the following spring, Johnston's strategy again was a deft, staged withdrawal that spared his outnumbered army and delayed the Union movement. Davis, though, demanded a more aggressive approach that would stop Sherman altogether and, certain he would never get it from Johnston, relieved the general in June. By the following February, the Union forces had smashed through Georgia and turned on the Carolinas, and Robert E. Lee reappointed

General Joseph E. Johnston

Johnston. This time, however, the Confederate commander could barely stall Sherman's advance, despite a valiant assault at Bentonville in March. Though Davis ordered him to continue the fight after Lee's capitulation, Johnston asked for an armistice on April 18 and formally surrendered on April 26, all but concluding the Confederacy's armed struggle.

He went on to enter the insurance business, served a term in the U.S. Congress, became a federal railroad commissioner, and wrote his memoirs. As a pallbearer at William T. Sherman's chilly winter 1891 funeral, Johnston refused to wear a hat out of respect for his former foe and died of pneumonia shortly after.

Kearny, Philip
1816–1862

The Union lost one of its most promising commanders when Phil Kearny was killed before the Civil War was even half over. Born into a distinguished New York family, he was steered away from a military career toward law, but when he received a million-dollar inheritance from his grandfather in 1836, he joined the Union cavalry. Kearny was sent to Europe to study the latest cavalry tactics, which the eager young officer put into practice fighting with the French in Algiers.

Returning to America, he served as aide-de-camp to Winfield Scott in the Mexican War, losing his left arm in battle. Kearny left the army after a stint in California but, longing for further military adventure, headed to Europe again in 1859. Joining Napoleon III's Imperial Guard, he was awarded the Legion of Honor for his service during the Italian Wars. With the outbreak of the Civil War, Kearny hurried back to the United States, and he was given command of a brigade whose uniforms he had adorned with a flashy piece of scarlet cloth known as the "Kearny Patch."

Already famous for his earlier military exploits, he won new acclaim during the spring 1862 Peninsula campaign in Virginia—and a promotion to major general—for his showing at Williamsburg, Seven Pines, and in the Seven Days campaign. Kearny also received attention when he vigorously protested George McClellan's decision to retreat at the conclusion of the campaign, claiming that "such an order can only be prompted by cowardice or treason."

Noted for riding into battle holding his reins in his teeth, Kearny cut a glamorous figure, which he matched with gallantry and fine fighting skills. He displayed those talents once again during Second Bull Run in August 1862, leading an aggressive, albeit unsuccessful, charge on Stonewall Jackson's left. Two days later, during heavy fighting around Chantilly mansion (Ox Hill), Kearny accidentally rode into enemy territory. Ordered to surrender, he was shot to death when he attempted to return to the Federal line.

Robert E. Lee, who admired Kearny and

General Philip Kearny

regretted the manner of his death, called a truce while his body was brought to Union officials, and personally sent Kearny's sword, horse, and saddle to his widow. As a tribute to its revered late general, the North issued the Kearny Medal and Kearny Cross, two decorations awarded for heroic acts performed by members of his former division.

Lee, Fitzhugh
1835–1905

Often confused with his first cousin, William Henry Fitzhugh "Rooney" Lee, General Fitzhugh Lee was the son of Sidney Smith Lee, arguably the favorite brother of Confederate General Robert E. Lee. He attended West Point two years behind his cousin Custis Lee and his lifelong friend Jeb Stuart; Fitz graduated forty-fifth in the class of 1856, and was assigned to duty on the frontier with the fabled 2nd U.S. Cavalry. In May 1859, he took an arrow shot in the chest at point-blank range while fighting Native Americans in Texas and was not expected to live. However, he survived with no apparent after-effects, and while recuperating was assigned to the position of assistant instructor of tactics at West Point. Several of his students would figure prominently in the war that was even then brewing; among them, Cadet George A. Custer would win fame as a Union cavalry brigadier, and Cadet John Pelham would die tragically at Kelly's Ford while serving as Jeb Stuart's brilliant artillery chief.

On May 3, 1861, Fitz Lee tendered his resignation following Virginia's secession from the Union; he immediately offered his sword to his native state and was made a first lieutenant in the Confederate Regular army. His first duty was as a staff officer to Joseph E. Johnston, with whom he saw the fighting at the First Battle of Manassas (First Bull Run). In August 1861, Fitz received command of the First Virginia Cavalry and was assigned to the cavalry corps under his friend Stuart. Serving in the same corps was his cousin William H. Fitzhugh Lee—who was saddled yet again with his childhood nickname of "Rooney," so as to lessen the confusion between the two of them.

After participating in the Peninsula campaign of spring 1862, and in the fabled Rides Around George McClellan, Fitz was promoted to brigadier general in July. Censured for not moving quickly enough to contain the advance of Union General John Pope's army in the Second Manassas (Second Bull Run) campaign in August, Fitz nevertheless redeemed himself in later campaigns; he was active at Antietam, and at Occoquan and Dumfries, Virginia. Fitz Lee was also of significant assistance to the Confederacy in the Chancellorsville campaign; it was he who discovered that the Union Army of the Potomac had failed to adequately protect their right wing, and Fitz led his men brilliantly to the assistance of General Stonewall Jackson when the Confederates decisively attacked the Union right to defeat General Joseph Hooker.

Unable to participate in the Battle of Brandy Station in June 1863, owing to a severe flare-up of arthritis to the extent that he could not ride, Fitz Lee was back in the saddle a few weeks later when Stuart's cavalry made their controversial roundabout ride to join the army in the invasion of Pennsylvania. He distinguished himself in the rearguard action on the third day of the Battle of Gettysburg, and in autumn of 1863, he was promoted to major general. Fitz Lee's gallant stand at Spotsylvania Court House on May 8, 1864, enabled the Confederate First Corps to seize what proved to be the key point of the battlefield and hold it against General Ulysses S. Grant's advance.

Grief-stricken at the death of Stuart a few days later, Fitz Lee entered into an unpleasant and perhaps uncalled-for wrangle with Wade Hampton over who should succeed Stuart in command of the cavalry corps. For a while, Robert E. Lee simply allowed his three senior cavalry commanders—Fitz, Hampton, and his own son Rooney Lee—to operate independently; when cooler heads prevailed in the squabble, Hampton received the corps command by virtue of his seniority. During part of that time, Fitz Lee was sent with his division to assist General Jubal Early in the Shenandoah Valley; on September 19, 1864, in the Battle of Winchester, Fitz's men were so heavily engaged against the enemy that their commander had three horses shot out from under him in the course of several hours of fighting, and he received a serious chest wound which incapacitated him until the first of the new year. By then Hampton had been reassigned to the Carolinas, in January 1865. Fitz technically received command of the cavalry, but did not effectively take command until the closing weeks of the war, when he was senior cavalryman in the Petersburg campaign.

Perhaps the least distinguished moment in his career was when he accepted an invitation to General Tom Rosser's shad bake and picnic on the morning of April 1, 1865. The Confederates under command of General George Pickett were spread over Five Forks, Virginia, a critical crossroads near Appomattox, with orders from General Robert E. Lee to "hold . . . against all hazards"; it was a major staging place for any action against the Union forces, and possibly the only line of retreat for the Army of Northern Virginia should disaster strike. Yet Fitz and Pickett both left the field and joined Rosser on the riverbank for a party, none of them having informed their subordinates that they were leaving, much less where they would be found in case of emergency. The Federals attacked in force under Philip Sheridan; Fitz's cousin Rooney was the senior officer on the Confederate line, but only directed the actions of his own cavalrymen, unaware that he could have called on all the cavalry and the infantry besides. Sheridan's men swept the Confederate position and took a commanding position across Five Forks, effectively cutting off any hope the Confederates could withdraw and regroup.

During the subsequent retreat toward Appomattox Court House, Fitz Lee did what he could to make up for his error by shadowing the Union army's every move, keeping an eye on them and reporting often to his uncle, the commanding general. When it became obvious that the Confederates were surrounded and surrender was likely their only option, Fitz got permission to take as many of his men as he could and make a break for North Carolina, where Joseph Johnston was attempting a last stand. However, Fitz realized before they had gotten very far at all that there was no use in even making the attempt; he turned his men around and surrendered his division at Farmville, Virginia, on April 11, 1865.

Fitz joined his extended family in Richmond, where not only his parents and his four brothers waited, but all of Robert E. Lee's family as well, in the crowded house on Franklin Street. Always a physically active man, Fitz decided the city and the house were too cramped for him to stay, and he headed out to Stafford County to try his hand at farming. Never one to let adversity get him down, he joked with friends that he had been a soldier all his life and was therefore accustomed to going to the army quartermaster to get his corn; now he was finding it hard "to draw it from the obstinate soil, but I did it!" He married in April 1871, and after several years of farming and trying various business ventures he found his true place: in politics. He was a very skilled public speaker, having as he did a cheerful, amusing nature and a natural gift as a storyteller; that and the fact that he was a Lee led in 1885 to election as governor of Virginia, a position once held by his famous grandfather, General "Light-Horse Harry" Lee of Revolutionary War fame.

When his term was over, Fitz then tried for election to the U.S. Senate, but failed to receive nomination from the Democratic party, of which he was a lifelong member. In 1896, Fitz was named consul general to Havana, Cuba, a post he held with great control and dignity in the face of a confusing series of ever more violent political problems, leading to the outbreak of the Spanish-American War in 1898. One of a few former Confederates who returned to Federal blue uniforms in this war (the other most prominent being perhaps Joe Wheeler), Fitz became a major general of volunteers, and received command of the 7th Army Corps, the frontline combat troops in the occupation of Cuba. He set his soldiers up at Camp Columbia near Havana, and took over peace-keeping duties after the capture of Santiago. Upon his return to the United States, Fitz Lee served from April 1899 until March 1901 as a brigadier general; he retired with that rank on March 2, 1901.

Besides his excellent military and political skills, Fitz Lee is also remembered for having written a charming, very readable biography of his famous uncle, Robert E. Lee; though amazingly full of odd inaccuracies for someone who had been so close to his subject, Lee's book is considered today to be one of the standard works on the life of the great general, and contains many family anecdotes that might otherwise have been lost to history.

Lee, Robert Edward
1807–1870

"His name might be 'Audacity,'" remarked a Southern colleague of Robert E. Lee. "He will take more chances and take them quicker, than any other general in this country, North or South." Facing an army larger and better equipped than his own, Lee was able to fashion, through sheer nerve and finesse, as well as dogged determination, several great victories for the Confederacy until forced to surrender at Appomattox. Indeed, his remarkable military skills as commander of the Army of Northern Virginia and as general-in-chief of the Confederate army kept the Confederacy fighting long after it had lost any chance to win the war.

Every ounce the Southern gentleman, Lee was strikingly handsome, charming, and, when not in one of his frequent fits of temper, exuded warmth and good humor. Devoted to his family and to the duty he felt toward his home state, Lee had a reputation for personal integrity that was second to none—a rarity in the heady politics-driven days of the Civil War. Union general Ulysses S. Grant, to whom Lee was finally forced to surrender, said of his battlefield opponent, "There was not a man in the Confederacy whose influence with the whole people was as great as his."

Lee came from a distinguished Virginia family. One ancestor, Thomas Lee, had served as royal governor of the colony; relatives Francis Lightfoot Lee and Henry Lee had been statesmen and soldiers during the Revolutionary War. His own father, Henry Lee, was known as "Light-Horse Harry" for his daring exploits as a cavalry commander during the American Revolution. "Light-Horse Harry," however, was an incompetent businessman who fled to the West Indies after plunging his branch of the family into debt.

Robert Edward Lee was raised by his mother, Anne Carter Lee, to whom he remained devoted until her death in 1829. Armed with a testimonial letter signed by five senators and three representatives—evidence of his powerful family connections—Lee entered the United States Military Academy at West Point in 1825. He graduated four years later, second in his class and without a demerit; his attention to his studies and his quiet demeanor earned him the nickname "the Marble Model." After graduation, he was appointed to the elite Corps of Engineers and spent more than 15 years engaged in several civil and military engineering projects largely involving the fortification of coastal defenses.

Except for the fact that the assignments took him away from his wife, Mary Ann Randolph Custis, and his growing family, Lee appeared to enjoy military life. Mary, a relative of Martha Washington, was a strong-willed, often bitter woman, who became crippled by arthritis. Nevertheless, the Lee marriage produced seven children. In 1836, Lee was promoted to first lieutenant; two years later, he was promoted again to the rank of captain.

At the outbreak of the Mexican War, Lee was stationed at New York Harbor. Although he objected to the expansionist aims of the war, he was anxious to prove his mettle as a soldier. First ordered to report to Brigadier General John Wool at San Antonio de Bexar, Texas, Lee was then assigned to General Winfield Scott's personal staff in Veracruz, Mexico. On several occasions during Scott's five-month campaign to secure the Mexican capital, Lee located key flanking routes that enabled Americans to outmaneuver and defeat a larger enemy, displaying strategy and tactics that would serve him well in the Civil War. At the victory celebration at the fall of Mexico City, Scott toasted the captain as the man "without whose help we would not be here." For his service, Lee received a brevet to colonel.

In 1852, he began a three-year term as superintendent of West Point, a position he served with distinction. He oversaw the extension of the academy's course of study from four to five years, increased the curriculum to include the study of strategy, and improved cadet discipline. Accepting the position of lieutenant colonel of the newly formed 2nd Cavalry Regiment in 1855, Lee spent most of the next several years in the wilds of Texas, fighting against Native Americans and Mexican bandits.

Then, in 1859, Lee took part in what many claim to be the opening salvo of the Civil War. Leading four companies of local militia and a handful of U.S. Marines, Lee captured John Brown after his Harpers Ferry Raid. Although opposed to both secession and slavery, Lee found he could not agree to fight against his home state of Virginia when offered command of the Union army in 1861. "I cannot raise my hand against my birthplace, my home, my children. . . ." he wrote. "Whatever may be the result of the contest I foresee that the country will have to pass through a terrible ordeal, a necessary expiation for our national sins."

Resigning from the U.S. Army, he accepted a brigadier general's commission in charge of all Virginia's military and naval forces after his state seceded in April 1861. By June 1861, Lee had supervised deployment of over 40,000 men and received a full general's commission on June 14. Unable to prevent Federal forces from taking western Virginia at the end of July, Lee then set out to put coastal defenses into place along South Carolina and Georgia.

On May 31, after Joseph E. Johnston was wounded in the Battle of Seven Pines, Lee took command of his army, which he renamed the Army of Northern Virginia (previously named the Army of the Potomac, not to be confused

General Robert E. Lee

with the Union's). From his first day of command, Lee faced what looked like an impossible task. Union General George B. McClellan had approached within seven miles of Richmond with 100,000 men, Union Major General Nathaniel Banks threatened important Confederate supply forces in the Shenandoah Valley, and Union Major General Irvin McDowell was encamped in nearby northern Virginia. In every instance, the Federals far outnumbered the Rebel forces opposing them. Lee believed the only viable solution was to combine his entire force against one of the threats, eliminate it, and thus dislocate the remaining Union forces. This approach formed an important corner-stone of Lee's strategy against the North throughout the war.

In a series of engagements that took place at the end of June, known as the Battle of the Seven Days, Lee forced McClellan back down the peninsula and away from Richmond. Taking the offensive, Lee then turned north to deliver another blow to the Union army in the battle of Second Bull Run at the end of August. At both Seven Days and Second Bull Run, Lee was assisted by the clever general, Thomas "Stonewall" Jackson. Jackson so admired Lee's abilities that he claimed, "I would follow him onto the battlefield blindfolded."

Having won two decisive victories, Lee continued his offense by preparing a northern invasion. His plan involved dividing his army as it advanced, each section then undertaking separate missions against the Union before reuniting in a main attack. Jackson was able to capture Harpers Ferry, but because a copy of Lee's plans fell into Union Major George B. McClellan's hands, Lee was forced to take up a defensive position at Antietam Creek, in Maryland. After fighting through the war's most bloody single day of battle on September 17, 1862, Lee was forced to retreat to Virginia.

Three months later, Lee redeemed him-self and his army in a surprising victory at Fredericksburg, Virginia. The Union attack by an army significantly larger than Lee's and led by Ambrose Burnside, took weeks longer than planned, allowing Lee to form strong defensive positions in the hills surrounding the town from which he was able to devas-tate his opponent. In May 1863, the deter-mined general forced another remarkable victory against a formidable enemy at Chancellorsville; although the battle was a strategic masterpiece expertly executed, it lost him his most precious corps comman-der, Stonewall Jackson.

Lee decided to attempt another northern invasion that summer, and by late June occu-pied the entire Cumberland Valley and other parts of Pennsylvania. Concentrating his forces at Gettysburg against new Federal com-mander George G. Meade, Lee lost his first major battle after three days of bitter fighting and was forced to retreat. The following spring, with just 60,000 men, Lee faced Union General Ulysses S. Grant and his 120,000-man Army of the Potomac for the first time.

During the Wilderness campaign, Lee was pounded by Grant's better-equipped forces in a series of battles. Finally, the Confederates were forced back into defensive positions at Richmond and Petersburg. To protect the cap-ital, Lee had to stretch his already depleted lines to meet Grant's continual encroachments on their right flank. As the Confederacy col-lapsed on other fronts, Lee's manpower short-age continued; in a one-month period, deser-tions claimed nearly eight percent of his strength.

In February 1865, although the Confederacy had clearly lost the war, Lee was placed in charge of all its armies. For three more months, he attempted to hold off the inevitable, but was finally forced to abandon Richmond in an effort to join his remaining 28,000 troops with those led by Albert Sidney Johnston in North Carolina. At Appomattox, however, he lost his final battle against Grant, to whom he surrendered on April 9, 1865. As Lee made his last ride down the lines on his famous horse, Traveller, he told his army, "Men, we have fought through the war together. I have done my best for you; my heart is too full to say more."

Although his home at Arlington had been confiscated by the Federals, he appeared to hold no bitterness for his former enemies and urged his fellow Southerners to accept the peace and rebuild their country. Lee chose to spend his last years as president of Washington College in Lexington, Virginia, where he established the nation's first journalism and business schools. Lee died on October 12, 1870, and was buried in the chapel he built on the campus of what was renamed Washington and Lee University after his death.

Lee, William Henry Fitzhugh "Rooney"
1837–1891

This youngest of the six Lee generals boasted by the Confederate army was the second eldest son of General Robert E. Lee. Born at his grandfather's estate Arlington, overlooking Washington, D.C. on the Virginia side of the Potomac River, William H. F. Lee is per-

haps better known to history as "Rooney" Lee, a nickname given him by his father because at his birth, the little fellow apparently resembled the black-haired, red-faced Irish gardener, one "Mr. Rooney." The nickname stuck to him the rest of his life, though there exists evidence in his younger sister's diary that he tried as early as age 15 to convince family and friends to call him Fitzhugh. Only his father seems to have achieved any success in that regard, for Rooney Lee served in the cavalry corps of the Army of Northern Virginia with his first cousin, Fitzhugh Lee, who had no other names from which to choose.

Rooney Lee attended Harvard University as a young man. He completed nearly all the four-year course of study, but gave it all up just shy of graduation because he was offered a post in the United States Army as a second lieutenant by his father's commanding officer and patriot, General Winfield Scott.

Sent out West, young Lieutenant Lee served creditably with the 6th U.S. Infantry under Albert Sidney Johnston in the Mormon Campaign. But when the campaign was over Rooney resigned his commission to marry his cousin, Charlotte Wickham, in 1859. The newlyweds settled down at an estate known as White House, which Rooney inherited from his grandfather; it had been the home of Martha Custis, Rooney's great-great grandmother, at the time of her marriage to George Washington.

The outbreak of the war in 1861 found Rooney Lee, now the father of his parents' only grandchild, uncertain of what to do. He felt in his heart that secession was wrong, but Virginia was his home—and like the rest of his family, he placed his sword in defense of Virginia when it sided with the South. He organized a cavalry company at the request of the governor and was appointed its captain; less than a month later he had been promoted to major and was assigned to command the cavalry under General William W. Loring. He was with the last male heir of the Washington family, Colonel John Augustine Washington, when the colonel was killed by Federal pickets in the West Virginia Campaign in the summer of 1861. That winter Lee was reassigned to Fredericksburg, where he was promoted to lieutenant colonel and made second in command of the 9th Virginia Cavalry regiment; very shortly thereafter he won the confidence of his men in the regimental election and became their colonel. The regiment was assigned to the cavalry corps under General Jeb Stuart, who remained Rooney Lee's commander until Stuart's death in 1864.

Through all the major campaigns of 1862 and early 1863, Rooney Lee's name appears in the records with great honor. He participated in all of Stuart's rides around George McClellan's army, during one of which his home was burned to the ground, and was at the Second Battle of Manassas (Second Bull Run); in the fighting before the battle of Antietam, Lee was injured and left unconscious in the street in an unusually confusing fight at Boonsboro, Maryland, when his horse fell on him during the action. He made his way back to the army under cover of darkness and was hailed by his comrades as if returning from the dead—for so he had been reported to be. Late in 1862, he was appointed brigadier general and received a cavalry brigade that included his old regiment. He

led this brigade through the Battles of Fredericksburg and Chancellorsville, to great credit in the reports of his superiors

At the beginning of the Gettysburg Campaign, Rooney Lee was severely wounded in the upper thigh at the Battle of Brandy Station, the largest cavalry battle ever fought on American soil, on June 9, 1863. He was taken to the home of his wife's relatives at Hickory Hill, near Hanover, Virginia, to recover; but while he was there, barely two weeks after his wounding, he was taken prisoner during a raid that was later found to have been planned specifically to capture him, in addition to its other objectives. The Union Secretary of War, Edwin Stanton, needed a hostage to use against the Confederate government, owing to an extremely unpleasant political situation. General Ambrose Burnside had captured a number of Confederate soldiers in Kentucky and, because they were wearing civilian clothing to supplement their meager uniforms, he had them hanged as spies. Outraged Southern commanders, calling this "military murder," captured some of Burnside's men in full uniform and had hanged them in retaliation. There were more hangings of Confederate soldiers, and casualties of this sort were traded back and forth until the Confederate government chose two officers from Libby Prison in Richmond, and notified Abraham Lincoln's government that the men would be hanged if any more Confederate soldiers died in this fashion. Stanton then made it clear he would do likewise: he chose Robert E. Lee's wounded son and one other officer as hostages for the good behavior of their government, and the matter came to a tense stand-off that lasted several months.

While Rooney Lee was thus awaiting the sentence of death, two remarkable things happened. A Union officer of some note, imprisoned at Richmond, asked a local clergyman to try and arrange a one-for-one exchange: he felt he could convince his government to trade Rooney Lee for him, if only General Robert E. Lee could be gotten to ask for the deal. The clergyman dutifully relayed the message and received a sad response: the commanding general would not ask for his own son what could not be asked on behalf of the lowliest soldier in his army. The minister later remarked that only one who knew how much Robert Lee loved his children could possibly have known how much such a decision had cost him. And in early December 1863, with Rooney's wife dying in Richmond, his brother, General Custis Lee, tried to arrange to take Rooney's place in prison, even if it meant dying in his stead, so his brother could come home for even a day to say good-bye to her. The Federal response, since the Burnside situation had not resolved, was that the fortunes of war had to remain with those upon whom they had fallen—and they refused the exchange. Charlotte Lee died on the day after Christmas.

Three months later, in March 1864, Rooney Lee was finally included in what proved to be one of the last official prisoner exchanges. Right afterward, U.S. government policy was changed: all Southern prisoners were to be sent North, in an attempt to prevent the Confederate army from having enough men in the field to defend their nation. Rooney returned to Stuart's command, promoted to major general—the youngest in Confederate service by one week's age difference—and went back to the fighting almost immediately. When Stuart was killed at Yellow Tavern in May, Rooney Lee and his fellow division commanders, Wade Hampton and Fitz Lee, each received independent command until arrangements could be made for one of them to succeed the much-lamented Stuart. Rooney led his division against the raid of Union General Wilson in June 1864, and was in command of the cavalry at the Battle of Globe Tavern in August.

At the end, in the desperate fighting of the Appomattox Campaign, Rooney valiantly tried to protect his father's starving army, joining his fellow cavalrymen in the heroic but vain attempt to be everywhere at once against the attacks of Union General Philip Sheridan. At Five Forks on April 1, 1865, Lee commanded the right wing of the Confederate forces—but was unaware of how many men he had to command, because his superiors, Fitz Lee and General George Pickett, had gone off to a shad bake with cavalryman Tom Rosser, and all three of them had failed to inform anyone of where they would be. In the closing days of the war, Rooney Lee was second in command of the Confederate cavalry in Virginia and was the only senior cavalry officer present at the surrender, Rosser having been captured, and Fitz Lee having broken away when the end seemed near, to attempt to join Joseph Johnston's army in North Carolina and make a last stand. One witness to the surrender described having seen numerous officers and men awaiting Robert E. Lee's departure from the McLean House, all of them deeply saddened at the tragic turn of events; sitting among them, tears streaming down his face, was Rooney Lee.

After the war, Lee returned to White House, built a new home, and settled down with a new wife to try and farm the land. He became president of the Virginia Agricultural Society and served in the state legislature as a representative from New Kent County from 1875 to 1879. Inheriting his great-uncle's plantation "Ravensworth" in Fairfax County, Rooney Lee moved back to the part of the state where he had been born, and in 1887 was elected to the U.S. Congress, when the former Confederate states received the right to vote once more. People came to him often with requests for assistance. He helped many families who had been left destitute by the war—both black and white—and once he filibustered on the House floor for several hours, making speeches and impassioned pleas, until Congress agreed to pay damages to the Virginia Theological Seminary in Alexandria, which had suffered a great deal of property and personal loss during the Union occupation. At that time he was told by an annoyed fellow congressman that he had the gentleman's vote in favor of the request, if he could tell them how the professors and clergy at the seminary had prayed during the war: for the president of the United States, or for the president of the Confederacy. Rooney's answer was: "They prayed for all sinners." The bill passed.

Shortly after being elected to his third term in 1891, Rooney Lee suffered a stroke following a lengthy illness. He was seriously ill throughout the spring and summer, and toward the autumn could barely speak; a friend said at the time that so highly did Virginians esteem him, it seemed the whole state was on its knees praying for his recovery. But on October 15—the twenty-first anniversary of his father's funeral—just around sunset, Rooney Lee died. He was buried first at Ravensworth, and then reinterred in the Lee Chapel crypt in Lexington, Virginia, where he rests today with his second wife and five of his seven children. He left behind him what was perhaps most important to the Lees, namely a reputation of honor, charity, duty, and responsibility.

Longstreet, James
1821–1904

"Old Pete" to his troops, the man Robert E. Lee called "my old war horse" may have been ineffectual in independent command, but despite the opinion of his detractors, he was a superb corps leader. Longstreet grew up in the deep South and graduated near the bottom of his class at West Point. Serving in the Mexican War and on the frontier, he became an army paymaster, and when he resigned from the U.S. military in June 1861, he hoped for a similar administrative post in the Confederacy. Instead, Longstreet, a master at field fortifications, was given command of a brigade, and after a solid showing at First Bull Run, he was promoted to major general.

Criticized for misconstruing orders at Seven Pines in spring 1862, Longstreet still emerged after the Seven Days Campaign as one of Lee's ablest subordinates and was placed in charge of an infantry corps. He played a key role in the Second Bull Run campaign in

August, holding back on the battle's first day, then successfully launching a crushing counterassault on the second. Instrumental at Antietam and Fredericksburg later in the year and promoted to lieutenant general, Longstreet was dispatched on an independent mission to the southeastern Virginia coast in April 1863, where he collected much-needed supplies but showed little initiative in confronting Union forces.

He rejoined Lee in time for the South's fateful invasion of Pennsylvania, about which, with his habitual preference for a tactical defensive position, he had great misgivings. Commanding the right wing at Gettysburg, Longstreet urgently counseled the Southern commander to maneuver the army between the Union troops and Washington and force the Federals to attack. But Lee remained on the offensive, and Longstreet's delay in launching the main assault on the battle's second day until the late afternoon is blamed by some for the Confederate defeat. Certain that it would fail horribly, he was even more reluctant to mount "Pickett's Charge" the following day and could barely nod the order to begin the doomed offensive.

With no bad feelings between him and Lee, Longstreet was sent west in September, where he reinforced Braxton Bragg's force in northern Georgia. Routing the Union army at Chickamauga, he was outraged that no follow-up attack on the vulnerable Federals was ordered, and demanded Bragg's removal. To ease tensions, Longstreet was given another independent command, assigned to retake Knoxville, Tennessee. His siege and attacks on the city were unsuccessful, how-

General James Longstreet

ever, and by April 1864, Longstreet was back serving under Lee in Virginia. During the chaotic Battle of the Wilderness, his troops accidentally shot him in the shoulder, and he was out of action until November. Returning to participate in the siege of Petersburg, he surrendered with Lee at Appomattox Court House in April 1865.

After the war, Longstreet became an insurance executive and scandalized the South by joining the Republican party. A longtime friend of Ulysses Grant (to whom he was related by marriage), he accepted several positions in the U.S. government, including minister to

Turkey. He also published his controversial memoirs, in which he dared to criticize—albeit judiciously—several aspects of Lee's command and defended himself against charges lingering since Gettysburg that his own actions in the decisive battle lost the war for the South.

Maury, Dabney Herndon
1822–1900

Dabney H. Maury was an illustrious son of a noted line of Virginians and one of the heroes of the Confederate Western theater. Descended from Huguenots who emigrated to America in the early 1700s, Maury was the great-grandson of Reverend James Maury, Patrick Henry's opponent in the famous "Parson's Cause" debates. His paternal uncle was the famed navy officer, oceanographer, meterological and hydrographic scientist Matthew Fontaine Maury, the "Scientist of the Seas," who also gave his time and talents to the Confederate States of America.

Born in Fredericksburg, Virginia, Dabney Maury first studied to be a lawyer at the University of Virginia. He discovered, however, that he loathed the law—and procured an appointment to West Point, graduating in the class of 1846 along with George Pickett—though significantly higher in the class standings. He served gallantly in the Mexican War as a lieutenant in the Mounted Rifles (later known as the 3rd Cavalry) and was given a brevet, or honorary, rank of first lieutenant for bravery in the siege of Cerro Gordo. That

brevet was later confirmed as a permanent rank, the first of many promotions Maury would earn for his bravery.

Between 1847 and 1852, Maury was back at West Point as an instructor of infantry tactics and a professor of geography, history, and ethics; after a four-year stint in Texas, he returned to the East, married, and became superintendent of the cavalry school in Carlisle Barracks, Pennsylvania. In 1859, he produced a skirmish drill manual for mounted troops; the next year, he was appointed assistant adjutant-general of the Department of New Mexico, and it is there the Civil War broke upon him. Immediately upon hearing of Virginia's secession, Maury resigned his commission, bade a tearful farewell to his friends, and returned to the East again; this was at Santa Fe in the first weeks of May 1861. On June 25, he was informed he had been dismissed from the service, "it having been ascertained to the satisfaction of the War Department that he entertained and had expressed treasonable designs." By that time, Maury had already secured a position as captain of cavalry in the Confederate army, more than amply proving to any military court where his loyalties had to rest.

By early 1862, Dabney Maury was a colonel and an aide to General Earl Van Dorn, commander of the Trans-Mississippi Department. On March 7 and 8, Maury was involved in the fighting at the Battle of Pea Ridge, Arkansas; for his bravery, he was made a brigadier general and was praised by Van Dorn as a courageous patriot.

For gallant service in the Battles of Iuka, Corinth, and Hatchie Bridge, Maury was promoted to major general on November 4, 1862; at Corinth, he attacked the Federal enemy with such force that he drove them through and out of the town, then harrassed them all through the later retreat. In July 1863, Maury was appointed commander of the district of the Gulf, taking command at Mobile; he defended the Gulf with all his capacity until the close of the war, when he was compelled to yield to overwhelming odds against him.

If such bravery were rewarded by fate, Dabney Maury would have spent the remaining years of his life in calm, plentiful retirement. But after the defeat of the Confederacy, Maury found his personal fortune gone, and the one thing for which he was best suited—military service—was denied to him as having been branded a traitor along with the rest of his Confederate comrades. He taught in various schools for a few years, then went into business on his own; during a yellow fever epidemic in New Orleans, he closed his business at a loss and volunteered as a nurse in the overcrowded hospitals of the city.

Maury was the founder in 1868 of the Southern Historical Society and a frequent contributor to their publication. He also wrote copiously, out of an apparent desire to keep the record straight. He published a history of Virginia for young people and wrote a witty, charming memoir entitled *Recollections of a Virginian* published in 1894. He was one of the organizers of the famed Westmoreland Club of Richmond, a band of famous Confederate Veterans who met for a while at 707 East Franklin Street—famed as the wartime residence of the Robert E. Lee family. Never one to forget his beloved army, Maury spearheaded a drive to improve the training and preparation of volunteer troops; he was also a member of the National Guard Association's executive committee for nearly 15 years. In the mid to late 1880s, Maury served his country once more, as minister to Colombia; offered a position as superintendent of the drawings of the infamous Louisiana Lottery, with a handsome salary, Maury refused the position as a matter of principle and was proven right when the lottery turned out to be an unmitigated disaster in which many Southerners lost all they had left.

Shortly after the turn of 1899, Dabney Maury passed away peacefully at the home of his son in Peoria, Illinois. He is buried in the Confederate Cemetery in Fredericksburg, Virginia, the town of his birth.

McClellan, George Brinton
1826–1885

"Just don't let them hurry me" may well have been the motto of the general hailed as the "Young Napoleon" at the beginning of the Civil War. Unwilling to take an aggressive approach and lead his men into battle, McClellan missed several opportunities to crush the enemy in the early stages of the war.

At first, McClellan appeared to be the best and the brightest of the Union army. Born into a wealthy Philadelphia family, McClellan earned high honors at the University of Pennsylvania in 1842. At the age of 16, he entered West Point and graduated second in the class of 1846, which voted him "most likely to succeed." Upon graduation, he was appointed brevet second lieutenant in the engineer corps and sent to the Mexican War. He distinguished himself at the Battles of Malan, Camargo, Tampico, and Vera Cruz; his performance at the battle of Cerro Gordo won him a brevet second lieutenant on April 24, 1847. "Gallant and meritorious conduct" at Churubusco and Chapultepec earned him the rank of captain.

From 1848 until 1852, he taught practical engineering at West Point, then was transferred to the West for another two years. In the spring of 1855, he was sent on a military commission to Europe to report on operations in the Crimean War; his report, *The Armies of Europe*, was published in 1861. Shortly after his return, McClellan resigned his commission and became a civil engineer in the railroad industry.

When the Civil War began, he was made major general of the Ohio Volunteers, commanding the Department of the Ohio. By the end of May 1861, he and his troops had pushed the Confederates out of western Virginia as far as the Alleghenies, in essence carving out the new pro-Union state of West Virginia. For his efforts, McClellan was made major general in the Regular army.

After First Bull Run, Lincoln called him to Washington and gave him command of what would soon be known as the Army of the Potomac. Although he appeared to have all the attributes of a great leader, including an aura of success emanating from his victories in Virginia, McClellan also had an alienating air of self-importance about him. When he received his command, he wrote to his wife, "Who should have thought, when we were married, that I should so soon be called on to save my country?"

In addition to his arrogance, McClellan had his politics: he was a Democrat—a War Democrat to be sure, but certainly opposed to Lincoln's Republican approach to the war. His politics put him up against many of his superiors, especially Secretary of War William Stanton.

McClellan devoted the summer of 1861 to organizing and training the army, spending eight hours or more a day drilling the men. Instilling discipline in his troops appeared to be his main objective: "Let an honest pride be felt in possessing that high virtue of a soldier, *obedience*," he wrote. His men, who had been humiliated at First Bull Run, came to adore their strong and optimistic commander. Despite having successfully prepared and equipped his 110,000-man army, McClellan refused to move against the Confederates at Manassas Junction and continue "on to Richmond." Claiming that the Confederates outnumbered him by tens of thousands, when in fact he had almost twice their strength, McClellan insisted he would not advance until he had at least 270,000 men. Whether McClellan truly believed himself outnumbered or whether he was, in fact, timid to the point of cowardice, remains a matter of debate. In any case, Lincoln denied him his request and strongly urged him to take action.

Although disturbed by the 34-year-old general's hesitancy, Lincoln remained confident enough in McClellan's abilities to promote him to general-in-chief of all the federal armies after Winfield Scott retired in October.

On January 27, 1862, Lincoln issued McClellan a direct command to advance through a document known as the President's General War Orders No. 1, issued on January 27, 1862. It took McClellan another two months, but he finally embarked on his brilliantly planned but poorly executed Peninsula campaign. His continued reluctance to seize the initiative allowed his superior army to be stopped by a much smaller Confederate force.

Despite winning several victories during Robert E. Lee's Seven Days campaign, McClellan was still convinced that the enemy outnumbered him and chose to retreat back to the Potomac by the end of July 1862. Frustrated with "Young Napoleon," as McClellan became known, Lincoln replaced him with Henry Halleck as general-in-chief, gave John Pope command of all Federal troops north and west of Virginia, and left McClellan in command, under Pope, of only the Army of the Potomac.

Just one month later, however, McClellan was back in charge after Pope was humiliated at Second Bull Run on September 1. As he had after First Bull Run, McClellan spent crucial weeks reorganizing his demoralized troops; then, instead of moving quickly to stop Lee's first invasion of the North, McClellan moved with typical caution, enabling forces under Stonewall Jackson to capture the Union garrison at Harpers Ferry in time to join Lee at Antietam. In fact, had Lee's battle orders not fallen into McClellan's hands in August, Lee's plan to capture Harrisburg, Pennsylvania, may have succeeded. Instead, McClellan forced a bloody showdown at Antietam on September 17, 1862. At the end of the day, when a final

Major General George McClellan

push against Lee may have completely crushed the rebel army, McClellan once again hesitated.

On October 1, Lincoln traveled to Sharpsburg to urge his commander to take the initiative. Later, he would make his request a direct order. Still, McClellan hung back. Finally, after nearly a month of inaction, Lincoln relieved McClellan of both commands, and the former golden boy of Lincoln's army retreated into civilian life.

Unable to fight on the battlefield, McClellan took up politics, where his charm and self-confidence appealed to many in his Democratic party, who nominated him for president in the Election of 1864. Confederate

Vice-President Alexander Stephens saw McClellan's candidacy as the "first ray of real light since the war began," as did many others in the South, but McClellan lost the election to Lincoln in a near-landslide.

Immediately following his defeat, he left on a three-year trip to Europe. He returned to the United States and reentered politics, serving as governor of New Jersey for one term in 1878. After leaving office, he resumed his work as an engineer. In 1887, he published *McClellan's Own Story*, a defense of his tactics during the war. He died on October 29, 1885.

success earned him promotion to captain on August 6, 1861.

For a short time, he served as an aide to Henry W. Halleck, then was transferred to Ulysses S. Grant's command in Tennessee as a lieutenant colonel. McPherson's top-notch engineering skills impressed the general. He gained Grant's trust by informing him of rumors perpetuated by Halleck and others pertaining to Grant's drinking habits. Grant's faith in McPherson was well-rewarded during the next several months, as he assisted in the captures of Forts Henry and Donelson, at the Battle of Shiloh, and the siege of Corinth.

McPherson, James Birdseye
1828–1864

Perhaps the most able Union soldier never to hold independent command, McPherson was instrumental in the Union victories at Forts Henry and Donelson, the Battle of Shiloh, during the Vicksburg campaign, and during William T. Sherman's Atlanta campaign, until he met his death on the battlefield at the age of 35.

Handsome, brilliant, and with easy good humor, McPherson was also one of the most well-liked men in the Union army. First in the West Point class of 1853, McPherson spent the beginning of his military career as a professor of engineering at his alma mater. When war broke out, his first assignment as a member of the Corps of Engineers involved improving Union harbors and seacoast fortifications; his

Major General James Birdseye McPherson

On May 1, 1862, McPherson was promoted to brigadier general; two months later, he rose to the rank of major general. In January 1863, just as Grant began to plan his Vicksburg campaign, McPherson was appointed commander of the 17th Corps in Grant's army. His skills as an engineer were in great demand as Grant realized the technical feat required to maneuver an army through the swamps and bayous of Mississippi. Once engaged in battle, McPherson's bravery and leadership were equally appreciated. His corps played particularly important roles in the capture of Raymond and Champions' Hill in May 1863.

When Sherman succeeded Grant as head of the Union forces in the West in March 1864, Abraham Lincoln put McPherson into Sherman's former position as commander of the 34,000-man Army of the Tennessee. McPherson and his army then played an important role in Sherman's Atlanta campaign. McPherson was particularly adept at accomplishing flanking maneuvers designed to crush the Confederate defensive lines. Although he was beaten back while attempting to stop Joseph E. Johnston's retreat at Snake Creek Gap, he succeeded in several other attempts.

His last battle took place on July 22, 1864. Attempting to maneuver around Confederate General John B. Hood's troops, McPherson and his men were ambushed by a surprise counterattack. In the confusion of the battle, McPherson, trying to cross from one column to another, instead rode into enemy lines, where he was killed by Confederate infantry. Sherman, it is reported, wept openly at the news of the brave young soldier's death.

Meade, George Gordon
1815–1872

Once referred to by his men as "a damned goggle-eyed old snapping turtle," the ill-tempered George Meade replaced Joseph Hooker as commander of the Army of the Potomac on June 28, 1863, just in time to lead it into battle at Gettysburg.

George Meade was born in Cadiz, Spain, where his father was a naval agent for the United States government. The Meade family moved back to the United States when Meade was about three years old; he received his education in Philadelphia and Washington. On September 1, 1831, he entered West Point and graduated in the top third of his class four years later. He resigned from the army a year after graduation in order to become a civil engineer. He reentered the army in 1842 as a second lieutenant in the Corps of Topographical Engineers and spent much of the following four years surveying various military sites, including Delaware Bay.

During the Mexican War, he was connected with the staff of General Zachary Taylor and saw action at Palo Alto and Resaca de la Palma. His first service of note took place at the Battle of Monterey, during which he led the advance on Independence Hill and earned himself a brevet first lieutenant. Serving under General Winfield Scott, Meade also participated at the Battle of Vera Cruz. Upon his return to the United States, Meade resumed his survey work for the Corps of Topographical Engineers.

In 1851, he was sent to the Florida reefs,

General George G. Meade

Gaines' Mills, and White Oak Swamp. In the latter battle, Meade was badly wounded and was forced to leave the army for a number of weeks. After a short period of recovery, Meade returned in time to lead his brigade in the battle of Second Bull Run; by the Battle of Antietam, less than a month later, he was in command of the whole division.

On November 29, 1862, he was made major general of volunteers in command of the 5th Corps. As its leader, he participated in the Battle of Chancellorsville on May 4, 1863, under Joseph Hooker. The badly injured Hooker seriously misused Meade's forces, pulling them back just as they assumed a strong position, but his men acquitted themselves well under the circumstances. At the close of the battle, which had been a surprising and devastating defeat for the Union, Hooker demurred in pursuing the Confederate army under Robert E. Lee, pleading to Lincoln for more troops.

Impatient with the lack of aggression displayed by yet another commander of the Army of the Potomac, Abraham Lincoln replaced Hooker with Meade, who had proved himself a dependable and capable leader. Unfortunately for Meade, Lee was attempting to consolidate his victory at Chancellorsville with a second northern invasion; it was now up to the irascible general to stop him. Just five days after he took command of the army, Meade faced the enemy at Gettysburg from July 1 to 3, 1863, the deadliest battle of the war. The Union managed to drive back the Confederate advance, but at great cost—more than a quarter of Meade's men had been injured or killed. Perhaps devastated by his losses and overestimating the

where he was engaged for five years in lighthouse construction, and in 1856 he was made captain of the corps conducting the geodetic survey of the Northern Lakes. At the opening of the Civil War, Meade was appointed brigadier general of volunteers in command of the 2nd Brigade of Pennsylvania reserves; as he gained in command and battle experience, he rose steadily in the military ranks.

In 1862, he saw action at Mechanicsville,

strength of his equally devastated enemy, Meade, like his predecessors at the head of Lincoln's army, failed to pursue the retreating Confederates aggressively. Nevertheless, Meade received a citation from Congress and was promoted to brigadier general in the Regular army on July 3, 1863.

During the summer and fall, Meade stayed close to Lee along the Rapidan Ring, planning to retake the ground between the Rapidan and the Rappahannock. Realizing the odds were against him, Lee withdrew south of the Rapidan on November 10, 1863, without a major battle. On November 26, Meade planned another offensive, this one aimed at Lee's right flank at Mine Run. His advance was slow, due largely to the ineffectiveness of his corps commander, William French. The languid pace gave Lee time to reinforce and extend his line, making an attack against the Confederates futile. Instead, Meade ordered his men to fall back. Although Meade was probably correct to avoid a battle he could not win, he again appeared to lack the battle-readiness necessary to defeat the tenacious Southerners.

Disappointed in Meade's performance, Lincoln promoted General Ulysses S. Grant to lieutenant general in charge of all the Union forces shortly after the Mine Run operation. Although Meade offered to resign, both Lincoln and Grant insisted he remain as commander of the Army of the Potomac. Grant would, however, move with Meade's army and, as his superior, largely control its actions. Throughout the rest of the war, Meade remained in Grant's shadow, carrying out his orders effectively and apparently without complaint.

On August 18, 1864, he was promoted to major general in the Regular army. Present at the Confederate surrender at Appomattox Court House, Meade was overjoyed at the war's end. Elisha Rhodes, a soldier from Rhode Island, described Meade as riding "like mad down the road with his hat off shouting 'the war is over and we are going home.'"

After the war, Meade commanded successively the Department of the East, the Military District of Georgia, and the Military Division of the Atlantic. He died of pneumonia, which was aggravated by the old war wounds received at White Oak Swamp, on November 6, 1872.

Morgan's Raids
OCTOBER 1862–JULY 1863

Confederate Brigadier General John Hunt Morgan's three spectacular cavalry raids in Kentucky and Tennessee so disrupted the Union army in the west that President Abraham Lincoln himself sent an urgent missive to commander Henry W. Halleck: "They are having a stampede in Kentucky. Please look to it."

John Hunt Morgan—the epitome of a cavalry commander sitting straight, tall, and fearless in the saddle—had served in the Mexican War but otherwise had no professional military training. He began his Civil War service as captain, incorporating the Lexington Rifles, a local militia he had organized in 1857, into the Confederate effort when the war began. By the end of 1862, he had been made a brigadier general in command of the 2nd Kentucky Cavalry and was serving under Major General Joseph Wheeler in the western theater.

Morgan's first raid undermined Union Major General Don Carlos Buell's attempts to capture Chattanooga, Tennessee. From July 4 to August 1, 1862, he and his men covered more than 1,000 miles, captured more than 1,200 prisoners, and destroyed several Union supply depots along the way. Morgan himself lost just 100 men.

Three months later, after serving under General Braxton Bragg during his Kentucky campaign, the clever horseman and his unit

Brigadier General John H. Morgan

joined Lieutenant General Kirby Smith as he attempted to retreat from Kentucky while under fire from pursuing Union troops. With 1,800 men, he circled eastward, captured Lexington, Kentucky, and destroyed Union transportation and communication lines before returning to Tennessee at the beginning of November.

Morgan's third raid, also known as his "Christmas Raid," was designed to help Bragg counter Union Major General William S. Rosecrans' advance through Tennessee. After organizing a division of two brigades totalling about 4,000 men, Morgan headed north from Alexandria, Tennessee, on December 21, 1862, to raid Rosecrans' lines of communication and supply.

Riding through Glasgow and Bardstown, he reached the Louisville & Nashville Railroad and followed it to Rolling Fork, near Elizabethtown, capturing the town and severing Rosecrans' lines.

By this time, the Union army had tracked the cavalrymen and were preparing to attack them as they headed back to Confederate lines. Morgan, realizing the danger, made his escape during the night with minimal loss of life, returning to camp on January 2, 1863. In just over a week, he and his men managed to destroy more than two million dollars worth of Union property and capture about 1,900 troops.

Morgan's final raid took place during July 1863. While his commander, Braxton Bragg, had directed him merely to slow Rosecrans' advance on Chattanooga, Morgan instead invaded Ohio. He hoped that a show of Confederate strength would raise support for the Southern cause among Yankees who were both tired of the war and sympathetic in some manner to the South. Although he did inflict damage on the Union supply lines, this raid appeared to more like a reckless adventure than a well-planned offensive.

On July 2, Morgan managed to elude more than 10,000 Union troops and took about 2,500 men across the Cumberland River. Wreaking his usual havoc on his way north, he joined in several skirmishes with Federals while completing the longest continuous march of the war, covering 90 miles in just 35 hours.

On the afternoon of July 13, he arrived in Harrison, Ohio, with a reduced force of 2,000 and with the Union already planning his capture. Indeed, his men had already captured 6,000 men, mobilized thousands of Union troops, destroyed 25 bridges, and demolished scores of railroads. By July 18, however, Morgan began to encounter serious enemy action; the next day, he was badly beaten by forces under Union Brigadier General Edward H. Hobson at Buffington Island. Supported by militia and gunboats, the Union troops managed to devastate Morgan's crew, killing about 120 and capturing another 700.

Morgan himself managed to escape with about 300 men and made a desperate effort to reach Pennsylvania. Hobson pursued relentlessly, finally capturing the wily horseman on July 26, at New Lisbon. Morgan and his raiders were then imprisoned in the Ohio State Penitentiary. Remarkably, Morgan was able to escape, although he was killed just about a month later during a cavalry encounter at Greeneville, Tennessee, on September 3, 1864.

Mosby's Rangers

Numbering about 800 at its greatest strength, this corps of partisan rangers sabotaged Union efforts in northern and western Virginia so successfully that historians believe they prolonged the life of the Confederacy for more than a year.

Formed in December 1862 by Confederate cavalry commander Jeb Stuart, the Rangers were made up of men on leave from army units, convalescents, and civilians unwilling to enlist in the Confederate army. Leading the men was the clever and fearless John Mosby (1833–1916). A diminutive man of just 125 pounds, Mosby had fought in the cavalry corps at First Bull Run, then joined Stuart's cavalry as a scout; Mosby originated the idea for Stuart's ride around Major General George B. McClellan's Union army during the Peninsula campaign. An impetuous, independent man—he became an attorney by studying for the law while in prison for shooting a fellow student at the University of Virginia— Mosby chafed under strict army rules.

After the Confederate Congress authorized the organization of partisan bands through the 1862 Partisan Ranger Act, Mosby convinced Stuart to give him an independent command. Mosby's Rangers operated from private homes and individual camps in western Virginia and only met as a group when Mosby called them together. Their military techniques were equally unconventional. They usually attacked in small groups in the dead of night, carried Colt .44 revolvers rather than swords or rifles, and more than once kidnapped Union officers and enlisted men after waking them from a sound sleep.

On March 8, 1863, Mosby and 29 of his men managed to capture Brigadier General Edwin Stoughton, two captains, and 30 enlisted men in the middle of the night in Fairfax Court House, Virginia. In addition, they also managed to garner 58 horses from the raid, the loss of which apparently upset Union President Abraham Lincoln more than the lost personnel. "I can make new brigadier generals," Lincoln remarked, "but I can't make new horses."

For the most part, Mosby's Rangers focused on attacking Union trains and supply depots, destroying them after appropriating their contents. In the summer of 1863, as Robert E. Lee made his second invasion of the North after his victory at Chancellorsville, Mosby and his men followed, undermining Union efforts to mount an effective counterattack. On June 10, shortly after hearing they had been officially designated the 43rd Battalion of Partisan Rangers, Mosby and his men rode into Maryland and burned a Union camp at Seneca Mills to the ground. "Mosby is an old rat and has a great many holes," wrote one of the many Union soldiers trying to put an end to the costly war of attrition Mosby was waging.

By August 1863, at least two prominent cavalry companies—the 2nd Massachusetts and the 13th New York—were ordered to pursue the clever horsemen on a full-time basis, but Mosby's Rangers remained elusive. In fact, just before and during Philip Henry Sheridan's Shenandoah Valley campaign of 1864–1865, the Rangers reached their peak in terms of manpower, activity, and effectiveness. On July 6, 1864, Mosby's guerrillas swooped down upon a camp at Mount Zion Church, killing 40 Union cavalrymen and taking about 60 others prisoner. Their attack several days later at Fairfax Station achieved nearly the same results, as did another outside of Falls Church a few weeks after that. In late summer, Robert E. Lee noted that during the previous six months alone, Mosby and his men had killed, wounded, or captured 1,200 Federals and had taken more than 1,600 horses and mules, 230 head of cattle, and 85 wagons.

During the fall of 1864, Mosby's Rangers continued to wreak havoc by upsetting Union plans to repair the vital Orange & Alexandria rail line at Manassas. The Rangers derailed trains, tore up tracks, and shot construction workers, so terrorizing Union forces that Secretary of War Edwin Stanton ordered that every house within five miles of the tracks be burned unless its owner was "known to be friendly." The threat was carried out, but the guerrillas continued their activities.

During the fall of 1864, Sheridan ordered Captain Richard Blazer to recruit 100 men and, equipping them with repeating rifles, led them on a search-and-destroy mission against Mosby's band. The "Gray Ghost," as Mosby was known, outmaneuvered Blazer on November 18; during a surprise attack, the Rangers killed or wounded all but two of Blazer's men and captured their weapons.

By the spring of 1865, the clever horsemen controlled a vast stretch of land between the Potomac and the Rappahannock known by friend and enemy alike as "Mosby's Confederacy." Hardly a day went by without a Ranger attack; even after word reached them of Lee's April 9, 1865, surrender at Appomattox

Court House, they continued to fight in the mountains.

After General Joseph E. Johnston's surrender about two weeks later, however, Mosby called his partisans together and urged them to surrender. Mosby, who had been wounded seven times during the course of the war, returned to Warrenton, Virginia, and practiced law until his death on May 30, 1916.

Pemberton, John Clifford
1814–1881

The man who was forced to surrender the Confederate stronghold of Vicksburg on July 4, 1863, was a Northerner by birth. Despite his heritage, however, Pemberton fought hard and well for the Confederate cause; his failure at Vicksburg was due more to the conflicting orders he received from his commanders, President Jefferson Davis and Joseph E. Johnston, than poor generalship on his part.

Pemberton was born into a family populated largely by antislavery, antiwar activists, including his father, who was a Quaker minister. Somehow drawn to the military in spite of his family's pacifism, his application to West Point was successful in large part because of a long-standing friendship between his father and President Andrew Jackson.

Pemberton graduated in 1833, twenty-seventh in his class of 50. Appointed second lieutenant and assigned to the 4th Artillery, he first served in the Seminole War in Florida from 1837 to 1839, then performed garrison duty until the opening of the Mexican War. Twice brevetted for gallantry at Monterey and Molino del Rey, Pemberton had advanced to the rank of major by the end of the war. His longheld pro-Southern and pro-states' rights opinions were further solidified upon his 1848 marriage to Martha Thompson, the daughter of a wealthy Virginia family.

On April 24, 1861, he resigned from the army to accept Jefferson Davis' offer of a brigadier general's commission. His first assignment was as commander of the relatively minor Department of South Carolina, Georgia, and Florida. Earning two promotions, one to major general and the second to lieutenant general, he remained in the post until October 14, when he was given command of the Department of Mississippi and Louisiana.

Considering his reportedly less than inspiring personality and lack of command experience, some military historians see this appointment as one of "Jefferson Davis' major mistakes." With approximately 40,000 men, Pemberton faced the armies of Ulysses S. Grant and William Tecumseh Sherman, who were determined to capture the city of Vicksburg, thereby opening the Mississippi River to the North and cutting the Confederacy in half. In the winter of 1862, Pemberton's first advance stopped Grant at the Battle of Chickasaw Bluffs, during which the Federal army lost some 1,700 men.

Grant embarked upon a new approach in the spring, and Pemberton received contradicting sets of orders from his commanding officers in response to the renewed offensive. Joseph E. Johnston wanted Pemberton to abandon the city and save his army, while

Jefferson Davis ordered Pemberton to hold the city at all costs. On May 14, Johnston sent word to Pemberton to come northeast and join him at Jackson, where he hoped they could defeat Grant together. Instead, Pemberton tried to stay close to Vicksburg and fight Grant from there. Just east of the city, Grant brought him to battle at Champion's Hill on May 16, beat him badly, and forced him back into Vicksburg with about 30,000 Confederates.

On May 22, the two-and-half month long siege of Vicksburg began. Pemberton watched his men grow ever more hungry and exhausted as Grant tightened his line around the city, cutting off communication and supplies. Finally, on July 3, Pemberton reluctantly gave the city over to the Federals, claiming that it would be "an act of cruel inhumanity to subject [the troops] any longer to the terrible ordeal."

Hoping to win easier terms of surrender, Pemberton shocked many Southerners by

General John C. Pemberton discussing the terms of surrender with Grant at Vicksburg.

agreeing to allow the Union to declare victory on the national holiday of July 4. Some accused Pemberton of treason, pointing to his Northern roots as further proof of his disloyalty, but no formal charges were ever brought. Pemberton's men were indeed allowed to resign from the army and return home rather than face Federal imprisonment.

Following the surrender of Vicksburg, no command could be given Pemberton commensurate with his rank; he therefore resigned and accepted appointment as a colonel of artillery. At the end of the war, he settled for a time at Warrenton, Virginia, but finally returned to his home state of Pennsylvania, where he died on July 13, 1881.

Major General George E. Pickett

Pickett, George
1825–1875

He neither ordered nor planned the assault, his troops comprised less than half of the attacking force, and the rest of his Civil War service was rather undistinguished, but because he spearheaded the gallant, doomed Confederate charge that climaxed the Battle of Gettysburg, George Pickett's enduring fame is assured.

Graduating at the very bottom of his West Point class, the elegant, almost foppish Virginian performed ably in the Mexican War and on the western frontier. After joining the Confederate army, he led the "Gamecock Brigade" in the Peninsula campaign, where he was seriously wounded during the Seven Days battles in June 1862. Though he was promoted

to major general that October and was present at Fredericksburg, Pickett saw little further action until Gettysburg.

Guarding the South's rear during much of the battle, he and his all-Virginian division did not arrive on the field until early the third day, July 3, 1863. James Longstreet, ordered by Confederate commander Robert E. Lee to mount an all-out assault on the center of the Union line, asked Pickett, one of his favorite officers, to coordinate the attack.

Eager to lead the South to glory, he confidently launched the charge with Longstreet's dubious nodded assent at about 3 p.m. Pickett stayed to the rear, as was customary for a division commander, while his three brigades and another six under A.P. Hill—a force totaling over 14,000—marched deliberately over three-quarters of a mile of open field toward the waiting Federals.

In less than an hour, Pickett's Charge was over, a magnificent effort but the disastrous failure that Longstreet predicted, with barely half of the attacking troops making it back to the Confederate line. When Lee told him to ready his division for a Union offensive, Pickett had to inform the general, "I have no division."

He continued to serve under Lee in the Petersburg campaign. On April 1, 1865, Pickett's troops were nearly wiped out at the Battle of Five Forks, presaging the fall of Richmond. After he was defeated again four days later at Sayler's Creek, Lee relieved him of his command just prior to the Appomattox surrender.

Once wanted by the Union as a war criminal for executing deserters, Pickett eschewed further military service—turning down a marshalcy from President Grant and a generalship from the Khedive of Egypt—to work in insurance back in Virginia. He never forgot the sad outcome of Pickett's Charge and, overlooking his own enthusiasm for the gamble, blamed Robert E. Lee. "That old man," Pickett insisted stubbornly and simply, "had my division massacred."

Polk, Leonidas
1806–1864

Having abandoned an early army career for the clergy, the Episcopal bishop returned to military service during the Civil War and rose

to high Confederate command, more through the support of his close friend, Jefferson Davis, than through his battlefield achievements.

Polk, a tall, gallant figure, came from a prominent North Carolina family and was a relative of President James K. Polk. Graduating from West Point near the top of his class, he left the army after six months to study for the Episcopal ministry. Polk was ordained as a deacon in 1830 and in 11 years was named bishop of Louisiana, where he owned a plantation and 400 slaves.

At the start of the war, Davis, a former West Point classmate, convinced the staunch secessionist that he would lend great prestige and legitimacy to the Southern cause by serving with the Confederate army. Bishop Polk was made a major general and assigned to supervise the fortification of the Mississippi Valley.

Determined to be more than a figurehead, Polk raced against Union officer Ulysses S. Grant to occupy the river stronghold of Columbus, Kentucky, in September 1861. In the process, however, he violated the border state's neutrality, causing its legislature to throw its support to the North. Placed under his West Point roommate Albert Sidney Johnston, Polk repelled Grant's attack on the citadel two months later and led four assaults against the Union general's troops the following April in the Battle of Shiloh.

As second-in-command to Braxton Bragg at Perryville, he was promoted to lieutenant general. Although Polk continued serving with Bragg, the two did not get along. After the New Year's 1863 Battle of Murfreesboro, Polk suggested that his superior be replaced, and nine

Leonidas Polk

months later Bragg was ready to court-martial him for his supposedly sluggish performance at Chickamauga. Standing behind his friend, Davis reassigned Polk to Mississippi, where, indeed showing a tendency for slowness, he was unable to stop the advance of William T. Sherman's forces from Vicksburg.

The bishop did not forsake his clerical work altogether during his Civil War service, taking time to baptize both John Bell Hood and Joseph E. Johnston and to perform celebrated raider John Hunt Morgan's wedding ceremony during lulls in the fighting. Leading a corps under Johnston during the 1864 Atlanta campaign, Polk was killed at Pine Mountain on June 14, by a stray round of enemy artillery fire while conferring with his commander. Jefferson

Davis considered his death one of the South's worst setbacks. But while Polk was well-liked and respected, not many other Confederates agreed with Davis' assessment.

Pope, John
1822–1892

A skilled and courageous commander, John Pope held command of the Union's Army of the Virginia (later the Army of the Potomac) just long enough to suffer defeat at Second Bull Run before being replaced by his predecessor, George B. McClellan.

Described by contemporaries as dashing and a fine horseman, Pope was also known to be arrogant, abrasive, and incapable of inspiring loyalty among his officers or troops. After graduating seventeenth in his West Point class of 1842, the former Illinois farmboy entered the Mexican War as part of the Corps of Topographical Engineers; for his actions there he was brevetted captain for gallantry. From 1846 until the opening of the Civil War, he worked as an army engineer in the West.

On May 17, 1861, Pope was appointed brigadier general of volunteers in Missouri, then given command of the Army of the Mississippi the following February. He and his army played a major role in the campaign to open up the Mississippi River to Federal navigation, helping to capture New Madrid and Corinth at the beginning of March 1862. Just a few weeks later, President Abraham Lincoln called the victorious and apparently aggressive young general east to take over the new Army of the Virginia, a well-equipped, well-trained army that George McClellan, a hesitant and ineffectual general, resisted sending into battle.

Pope's first action was to issue a high-handed, condescending statement that alienated officers and soldiers alike. Addressed to his troops, the statement suggested that McClellan, whom the troops adored and whose dismissal outraged the ranks, had taken a faulty approach to the war and that the soldiers themselves had not performed well. Pope also encouraged his men to seize food and supplies from Virginia farms and suggested that anyone suspected of aiding the Confederacy be hanged for treason without trial. Such opinions earned him the enmity of some of the more circumspect Northerners and certainly that of every Southerner, including General Robert E. Lee, who described Pope as a "miscreant."

That Pope entered the eastern theater at a time when the Confederates had the upper hand did not help matters, either. After pushing the Federals back from Richmond during the Seven Days Campaign in the spring, Lee made a daring move to invade the North. Lee's brilliant strategy simply overwhelmed the relatively inexperienced commander. When the armies met from August 28 to September 2, Lee's 55,000 troops outmaneuvered and outfought Pope's Army of the Virginia at Second Bull Run. The next day, Lincoln removed Pope from command, replacing him with the problematic but beloved "Little Mac" McClellan.

Pope's Civil War career effectively ended; he was sent to command the Department of the Northwest, where he became somewhat of an expert in Indian affairs. Promoted major general in the U.S. Army in 1882, Pope retired four years later. He died at the Old Soldiers' and Sailors' Home in Sandusky, Ohio, September 23, 1892.

Porter, David Dixon
1813–1891

By the time the Civil War began, 48-year-old David Porter, soon to become one of the greatest naval heroes of the war, had been engaged in naval affairs for more than 35 years.

A member of the most distinguished family in United States naval history, David Dixon Porter literally grew up on the sea. At the age of 10, he accompanied his father, a naval officer and diplomat, on an expedition to suppress piracy in the West Indies. At the age of 14, he was made midshipman in the Mexican Navy. In 1829, Porter returned to the United States and joined the navy, serving in the Mediterranean and the South Atlantic. First as lieutenant and then as commander of the *Spitfire*, Porter took part in every coastal engagement during the Mexican War from 1846 to 1848.

On April 1, 1861, he was given command of the powerful steamer *Powhatan* and sent to the Gulf of Mexico, a promising start to his Civil War service. As commander of the *Powhatan*, Porter sailed to the Gulf of Mexico to relieve Fort Pickens at Pensacola, Florida, which had been under siege for several months. He stayed in the gulf for the remainder of the war's first year.

To assist David Farragut's assault on New Orleans in April 1862, Porter led a flotilla of small sailing vessels, equipped with mortar and shells, into the harbor in hopes of diminishing Forts Jackson and St. Philip. His plan failed, however, and Farragut's larger, more powerful fleet was necessary to take the forts; the forts finally surrendered on April 28, 1862.

Two months later, Porter was appointed acting rear admiral of the Mississippi Squadron and assumed naval responsibility for the Mississippi and its northern tributaries. His first action, taken in cooperation with William Tecumseh Sherman, was to capture the Arkansas Post in January 1863, thereby opening the Mississippi to Federal navigation. In the spring, Porter assisted Ulysses S. Grant in his move against Vicksburg. In one attempt to reach the city, Porter sailed his fleet from the Mississippi through Steele Bayou, then into and across the Yazoo River below the heavily fortified Fort Pemberton. Porter's gunboats, however, were caught in the narrow, swampy streams that crisscrossed the region. When Confederates began felling trees behind the fleet in an attempt to trap the Union ships, Porter was forced to call to Sherman for army support. Once extricated, Porter headed back to the Mississippi, his first mission at Vicksburg a failure.

On April 30, however, he came through for Grant by taking a dozen vessels loaded with supplies and soldiers across the Mississippi through heavy Confederate gunfire. The pas-sage took more than two hours, but Porter managed to lose just one transport. For his actions at Vicksburg, he was promoted to rear admiral and given increased responsibility for a larger territory: the Mississippi River system north of New Orleans.

The spring of 1864 found Porter ready to undertake what was to be a dreadful failure for the Federal forces during the Red River Campaign. Nature and poor planning scuttled the mission to secure the important river for the Federals. Porter nearly lost his fleet during the expedition, but managed to save most of his ships. In October 1864, Porter was sent east to take command of the North Atlantic Blockading Squadron, which was responsible for blockading the coast north of South Carolina. Under orders from Grant to capture Fort Fisher at Wilmington, Porter and army Brigadier General Alfred H. Terry planned a combined naval-land offensive.

On the morning of January 14, 1865, Porter's fleet of 40 warships—the largest ever assembled—began to bombard the fort. At 4:00 p.m., 1,600 of Porter's sailors and 400 marines stormed the northeastern end of the fort while brigades of infantry scaled the parapet. Fierce hand-to-hand combat continued for several hours, until the garrison finally fell at 9:00 p.m., closing the Confederacy's last open port on the East Coast.

After his victory at Fort Fisher, Porter's Civil War career ended, but he continued to serve in the military for the rest of his life. He was promoted to vice-admiral in 1866 and to admiral in 1870. He served as superintendent of the Naval Academy for several years before being appointed head of the Navy Department. David Dixon Porter's remarkable life-long record as a naval officer appeared to run in the Porter family. David Farragut, under whom he served at the capture of New Orleans, was his foster brother. Another brother, Commodore William D. Porter, assisted Andrew H. Foote as commander of the *Essex* in the campaign up the Tennessee River early in 1862. Porter's cousin, Fitz-John Porter, another promising Civil War officer, won accolades for his performance as a soldier during George McClellan's Peninsula Campaign, but gained many detractors after Second Bull Run. Author of several books about his remarkable life, Porter remained active until his death at the age of 78.

Porter, Fitz-John
1822–1901

The story of Union General Fitz-John Porter must surely rank as one of the most frustrating and difficult in the annals of the war. Born to a Portsmouth, New Hampshire, navy family that included Commodore David Porter and Admiral David Dixon Porter, young Fitz-John nevertheless chose the army, graduating from West Point high in his class in 1845. He served for a time in the 4th Artillery, until the outbreak of the Mexican War took him to that training ground for future Civil War generals. Serving under Zachary Taylor, Porter was later transferred to Winfield Scott's army, with whom he saw action from Vera Cruz to Mexico City.

He was brevetted for gallantry at Molino del Rey and Chapultepec, and finished the war with a rank of major.

From 1849 to 1855 he was an instructor at West Point, teaching artillery and cavalry tactics. Eventually returning to more active service, Porter was involved in the 1857 Mormon Expedition to Utah, where he served with many men who would later fight alongside or opposite him in the Civil War. On the eve of the nation's breakup, Porter was assigned to numerous difficult tasks associated with the secession of the Confederate states: inspecting Charleston's defenses, lest it should become necessary to level them; finding the means to withdraw loyal troops from Texas after that state's secession; and keeping the trains running between Washington City and the Northern states.

When the fighting began, Porter received a number of assignments, including an appointment on May 17 as brigadier general of Volunteers, and was sent to fight with Nathaniel Banks and Robert Patterson in the Shenandoah Valley. During George McClellan's Peninsula campaign, Porter, who was initially an intimate of McClellan, rose from division command under General Heintzelman to command of the 5th Corps. Attacked in force at Mechanicsville and Gaines Mill, Virginia, during the drive to take Richmond, Porter offered a valiant defense of his position; after a hard fight, he withdrew in good order across the Chickahominy River. Porter's corps was responsible for the safety of the wagon train as McClellan finally began moving across the peninsula, and had orders to occupy and hold Malvern Hill as a protec-

General Fitz-John Porter and staff, June 1862.

tive point for the entire Union army in the campaign.

McClellan's troops were later reassigned to Major General John Pope, in the Union entity known as the Army of Virginia. Porter's men reached the rendezvous by way of the Rappahannock River at Falmouth, Virginia— just in time to receive the brunt of a startling attack by Robert E. Lee and Stonewall Jackson, as they moved Jackson's corps in an attempt to skirt Pope's right flank and break for Thorofare Gap. It took Pope some time to realize what was afoot, whereupon he sent Porter to try and contain the elusive Jackson before he could reunite with the rest of Lee's army. The plan was to attack Jackson's right flank on August 29, 1862, and defeat him before turning to deal with James Longstreet,

but Porter failed to follow through on this task. At Second Bull Run (Second Battle of Manassas), Jackson was able to decisively defeat Pope on the old familiar battlefield, sending the scattered and demoralized Northerners back to Washington, D.C., where the army was reshuffled and Porter's corps was returned to McClellan's command.

The following November, General Porter was relieved of command and summoned to a court martial; the charges, leveled by John Pope, included failure to obey orders, disloyalty, and misconduct in the face of the enemy, any one of which was a serious charge all on its own. Pope was clearly looking for a scapegoat, and though Porter offered a rigid defense along the lines that Pope had not given clear orders at any time, and that the Confederates had been in such position as to render impossible the orders he did receive, he was found guilty and dishonorably dismissed from the army on January 21, 1863—coincidentally the thirty-ninth birthday of Stonewall Jackson, the author of Porter's troubles.

Porter began immediately trying to clear his name, but was unable to secure a review of the proceedings until 1879. The wait was worth it, for a board of generals appointed to look into the matter found in Porter's favor. However, it was not until 1882 that the president took some action on Porter's behalf; part of the sentence was remitted to allow him to hold office in the United States. During this time, Ulysses S. Grant wrote an unsolicited testimony in Porter's favor, publishing an article in the *North American Review*, "An Undeserved Stigma." Four years later, on August 5, 1886, ironically owing to the intervention of Congressman Joseph Wheeler, formerly a Confederate cavalry commander in the Army of Tennessee, Porter was reappointed to the rank of colonel of infantry from May of 1861—unfortunately without remuneration of back pay—and then was promptly placed on the retired list two days later.

Porter was finally able to get on with his life and moved to Colorado, where he was involved in mining. He had not been entirely idle during the years that he spent waiting for exoneration, however; he ran a mercantile business in New York, and reluctantly turned down an offer from the Khedive of Egypt of command of the entire Egyptian Army. Porter held such disparate positions as construction superintendent for the State Asylum in New Jersey; receiver of accounts for the Central Railroad of New Jersey; and public works, fire and police commissioner for the city of New York. At the age of seventy-nine, General Porter died of natural causes in Morristown, New Jersey, leaving behind a widow and four children.

Scott, Winfield
1786–1866

Having already served as the country's general-in-chief for two decades, America's preeminent military figure—perhaps the most celebrated since George Washington—was nearly 75 when he commanded the Union armies at the start of the Civil War. By that time, Scott, a Virginia native who refused to join the Confederacy, was clearly nearing the end of his brilliant career.

Hero of the War of 1812 and Black Hawk War, commander of U.S. forces in the Mexican War, unsuccessful Whig presidential candidate in 1852, Scott, called "Old Fuss and Feathers" because of his devotion to military pomp and protocol, now suffered from gout and vertigo, weighed more than 300 pounds, and could no longer ride his horse. Because of his infirmities, he required a field commander and urged Lincoln to appoint his fellow Virginian Robert E. Lee to the position. George B. McClellan, who got the post after Lee turned down the Union commander's personal appeal, soon began to resent Scott and took to contradicting him in staff meetings and snubbing him in public.

By then, however, the general-in-chief was

General Winfield Scott (seated)

retired to write his two-volume memoirs, travel through Europe, and see the essential elements of his Anaconda Plan ultimately prove effective in the waging of the war.

Shaw, Robert Gould
1837–1863

Dubbed "the blue-eyed Child of Fortune" by philosopher William James, Robert Gould Shaw—the son of wealthy Boston abolitionists—reluctantly became the commanding officer of the 54th Massachusetts Regiment, the first Northern regiment comprised of free black soldiers and noncommissioned officers, led by white ranking officers.

Shaw was a Harvard man from a period when Henry Adams, grandson and great-grandson of presidents, and William H. F. Lee, son of Confederate commander Robert E. Lee, also attended the school. He had seen some combat before accepting a new assignment at the urging of his mother: to train and lead a regiment of free blacks. Though not particularly in sympathy with abolitionist goals, the young white commander—he was barely twenty-six when he took command—began to respect the courage and resolve of his untrained soldiers.

Many people believed at the time that black men were not brave enough to withstand combat, and though Shaw's correspondence shows he had some anxiety along that line, nevertheless he continued to build the 54th into a trained fighting unit.

being amply ridiculed elsewhere as well. Blamed for the Union's dismal showing in the first months of the war, Scott received sharp criticism for his "Anaconda Plan," in which he recommended a naval blockade to press the Confederacy while the Union gradually developed its armed forces for what he anticipated to be a long struggle. Although Scott was more clearheaded on the subject than the majority of military and political figures—Union and Confederate alike—who believed the war would conclude quickly, many suspected Old Fuss and Feathers was growing senile.

On November 1, 1861, after another Union battlefield defeat at Ball's Bluff, Lincoln accepted Scott's standing offer to resign. Succeeded the same day by McClellan, he

Their first major fight was almost their last, and certainly was the end of Shaw; the 54th was assigned on July 18, 1863, to make an impossible assault on Fort Wagner, one of the harbor defenses of Charleston, South Carolina. Shaw led the attack on foot, and made it as far as the parapets before he was shot dead. At least twenty of Shaw's men were killed by his side, but they had reached the fort itself, and forever laid to rest the belief that former slaves would not fight for their freedom.

Shaw and his comrades were buried in a trench grave, almost where they had fallen. When it was suggested that he bring his son's remains home to Boston, Shaw's father refused, saying Robert was where he belonged: in the same grave with the gallant men he had commanded.

With doubts quelled as to the courage of the freedman, the North incorporated more than 50 new black regiments before the end of the year.

Sheridan, Philip Henry
1831–1888

One of the youngest commanders to serve in the Civil War, Philip Sheridan was known for both his extraordinary skills as a cavalry commander and his uncompromising attitude toward the enemy. "Smash 'em up, smash 'em up!" he would urge his calvary before they embarked upon one of their many devastating raids through Southern territory during the course of the Civil War.

Sheridan fought in several important bat-

tles in both the Western and Eastern theaters of the war, but was best known for the "scorched earth" policy he followed during his infamous Shenandoah Valley campaign (Sheridan's) from 1864 to 1865.

The son of Irish immigrants, Sheridan was born in Albany, New York, and brought up in Ohio. Too young to serve in the Mexican War, Sheridan was nonetheless so eager to pursue a military career that he falsified his birth date by one year to gain early admittance to West Point in 1848. Just five feet five inches tall and barely 115 pounds, this whip of a man was known as much for his bad temper as his fine horsemanship and fighting spirit. In fact, he was nearly expelled during his first year at the academy for attacking a cadet officer with a fixed bayonet during an argument. After serving a one-year suspension, Sheridan was allowed to return.

He graduated from West Point in 1853, thirty-fourth in his class of 49 members. His first assignment, as brevet second lieutenant in the 3rd Infantry, took him to the Rio Grande in Texas in 1854; he was transferred a short time later to the 4th Infantry in the Northwest. In 1861, Sheridan was promoted to first lieutenant, then captain of the 13th Infantry. Following the fall of Fort Sumter, he worked as chief quartermaster and commissary of the army in Southwestern Missouri until May 1862, when he was promoted to colonel of the 2nd Michigan Cavalry under Henry Halleck during the campaign for Corinth, Mississippi. Although he also acted as quartermaster— keeping track of supplies for the camp—during this period, his performance at Corinth marked the turning point of his career. Just a month later, at Boonesville, Mississippi, he and his troops experienced their first victory. The triumph at Boonesville earned him the rank of brigadier of volunteers in October, as well as a transfer to the 11th Division of the Army of the Ohio, enabling him to participate in the Battle of Perryville. At Murfreesboro on December 31, 1862, his division of 5,000 held back more than twice that number of troops under Confederate General Braxton Bragg, allowing Sheridan's commander, General William Rosecrans, to form new lines and finally defeat the enemy.

As major general of volunteers, to which he was promoted on March 16, 1863, Sheridan participated in the capture of Winchester and assisted in the battle of Chickamauga in September, where his division sustained terrible losses at the hands of James Longstreet. At Chattanooga, Sheridan not only broke the Confederate line by storming Missionary Ridge, he also almost succeeded in capturing Braxton Bragg and several of his generals. By the end of the battle, his division was the only Union force able to pursue the retreating Confederates.

Impressed with Sheridan's stamina, bravery, and ruthlessness, General Ulysses S. Grant selected "Little Phil," as he was now known by his men, to head the cavalry corps of the Army of the Potomac. In that capacity, he participated with Grant in the Battle of the Wilderness and at Spotsylvania. From May 9 to 24, 1864, he undertook what became known as "Sheridan's Richmond Raid." His goal during this campaign was to destroy his counterpart at the head of the Confederate cavalry, the equally clever and daring Jeb Stuart. In addition, he hoped to raid the city of Richmond, damaging its communications

Major General Philip H. Sheridan

and supply lines. Sheridan's first independent cavalry action was successful on both counts: on May 11, Sheridan defeated Stuart, mortally wounding him at the Battle of Yellow Tavern. By the time he returned to Grant on May 24, he had ridden completely around Lee's army, severed many vital communication lines around Richmond—including 10 miles of railroad track on three different lines and its telegraph system—and captured vast quantities of supplies.

In August 1864, Grant made the now famous Sheridan commander of the new Army of the Shenandoah. In this capacity, his primary objectives were to stop Jubal Early, who had made several raids on Washington, D.C., and to decimate the Confederate bread basket of the Shenandoah Valley. By August 7, Sheridan's Shenandoah Valley campaign was underway. Seven months later, Early had retreated and the once fertile valley lay in ruin. Sheridan's actions during this campaign earned him the undying enmity of the Southerners and two promotions from the Northern army, the first to brigadier general in the Regular army in September and the second to major general on November 8. By the spring of 1865, the Siege of Petersburg was nearing its final days.

On April 1, when Union commander Gouvernor Warren miscalculated the Confederate position at the Battle of Five Forks, Sheridan's quick thinking managed to transform what might have been a devastating loss into a resounding victory. Sheridan was able to readjust his cavalry divisions in time to turn the Confederates back and force a surrender. Sheridan captured four cannon, eleven flags, and about 5,200 Confederates. He and his troops were present at Appomattox Court House when Grant accepted Robert E. Lee's surrender.

Following the war, Sheridan served as commander in various departments throughout the country, including in the Department of the Gulf and the Department of the Missouri. In early 1869, he was placed in command of the Military Division of the Mississippi during Reconstruction. His unforgiving treatment of Southerners, so effective in war, was counterproductive in peace, and he was removed after just six months.

When Grant became president in 1869, William Tecumseh Sherman was elevated to general-in-chief and Sheridan was promoted to lieutenant general. During the 1870s, he spent much time in Europe and was present in Germany during a portion of the Franco-

Prussian War. When Sherman retired in 1883, he left Sheridan his successor as general-in-chief of the United States Army. He was promoted to full general June 1, 1888, just two months before he died in Nosquitt, Massachusetts, on August 5, 1888.

Sherman, William Tecumseh
1820–1891

"War is cruelty," wrote Sherman, one of the Union's most valuable generals and Ulysses S. Grant's most trusted subordinate. "There is no use trying to reform it. The crueler it is, the sooner it will be over." Both brilliant and unstable, Sherman was instrumental in several early campaigns in the West, but is best known for the ruthless execution of his Atlanta campaign, March to the Sea, and Carolinas campaign in the final year of the war. Many military historians consider that Sherman's policy of destroying property and undermining the lives of civilians in order to end the war sooner and with fewer casualties makes him the first practitioner of modern warfare.

Sherman was born in Ohio and, orphaned at a young age, raised by Thomas Ewing, a U.S. Senator and cabinet member. After obtaining an appointment to West Point through the efforts of his foster father, Sherman graduated sixth out of 42 in the class of 1840. He was appointed second lieutenant in the 3rd Artillery and first served in Florida and at Fort Moultrie, South Carolina.

From 1843 until the start of the Mexican War, his military activities caused him to travel extensively in the South. One expedition took him down the Mississippi River and across Georgia, and another took him on a three-month tour of Southern states. The knowledge of Southern geography he gained during his early years in the army would serve him well during the Civil War. During the Mexican War, Sherman acted as an aide to Captain Philip Kearny and then as adjutant to Colonel Richard B. Mason in San Francisco, California, for which he was brevetted captain. Following the war, Sherman was discouraged by the lack of advancement—and excitement—available during peace time and resigned his commission in 1853. He returned to San Francisco to work for the St. Louis-based banking firm of Lucas, Turner & Co.

Sherman managed the company's finances well, particularly during the financial crisis of 1857, but the bank nevertheless failed at the end of that year. The restless Sherman then practiced law and real estate in Fort Leavenworth, Kansas, until he was appointed superintendent of the Louisiana State Seminary of Learning and Military Academy near Alexandria, Louisiana—the forerunner of Louisiana State University at Baton Rouge.

Although Sherman developed a strong affinity for the South and was offered a commission in the new Confederate army when Louisiana seceded, he believed that a strong union was best for the country and so returned to his wife and children in Missouri. Disgusted by the failure of Congress to circumvent the crisis, Sherman wrote to his brother, Senator John Sherman of Ohio, "You [politicians] have got things in a hell of a fix . . . I am going to St. Louis to take care of my family, and I will have no more to do with

Major General William Tecumseh Sherman

it." Taking a job as the president of a St. Louis streetcar company, Sherman did just that for several months, until finally returning to the army to accept an appointment as colonel in the new 13th Infantry on May 14, 1861.

By July, Sherman had been given command of a brigade, consisting of the 13th, 69th, and 79th New York, in Irvin McDowell's army enabling him to participate in First Bull Run. Although the Union army was defeated there, Sherman's troops fought with more discipline than most, which earned him a promotion to brigadier general of volunteers on August 2, 1861. Sent to Kentucky as second-in-command to Robert Anderson, Sherman assumed command when Anderson fell ill.

Ordered to invade eastern Tennessee, Sherman showed his first signs of mental and emotional instability when he insisted he needed at least 200,000 men to do so, a request that prompted George B. McClellan to conclude that "Sherman is gone in the head." Sherman was quickly replaced and sent to Missouri, where he assumed command of the District of Cairo under Henry Halleck. Although his emotional strength would always be questioned, his military skills redeemed him in the eyes of his commanders.

His performances at Shiloh, where he was wounded but refused to leave the field, and at the siege of Corinth earned him a promotion to major general of volunteers. After Halleck was made general-in-chief of the Union armies, and Grant assumed command in the West, a strong and lasting friendship between Grant and Sherman developed. It was Sherman who convinced Grant not to resign after being passed over for the promotion given to Halleck; Grant remained a staunch Sherman supporter despite rumors of Sherman's instability. Later, Sherman would write of the friendship, "Grant stood by me when I was crazy and I stood by him when he was drunk; and now we stand by each other always." Both of them West Pointers with a fondness for cigars, the two would form an unbeatable team over the coming years.

Grant first sent Sherman to Memphis to establish the city's defenses, then prepared to use him in his Vicksburg campaign. In the first Vicksburg offensive at the end of December 1862, Sherman was ordered to assemble his troops and, assisted by gunboats commanded by David Dixon Porter, move down the Mississippi River. Caught in heavy swamp water, the gunboats were attacked by Confederate batteries at Chickasaw Bluffs, leading

to a humiliating defeat. President Abraham Lincoln then ordered Sherman to relinquish command to John A. McClernand, who assigned Sherman leadership of the 15th Corps. Sherman participated in the successful Union offensive against Arkansas Post, a Confederate fort about 115 miles south of the state capital on the Arkansas River.

Following this victory, both Sherman and McClernand were ordered to assist Grant—as equals—on his spring campaign to take Vicksburg, which led to the city's fall on July 4, 1863. Sherman, who was responsible for taking the hills overlooking the Yazoo River and thus assuring Grant reinforcements from the North, was appointed brigadier general in the Regular army for his actions. In the fall of 1863, Sherman was ordered to assist William S. Rosecrans at Chattanooga. By holding his ground during the fierce battle at Mission Ridge, Sherman allowed George Henry Thomas to take the ridge and thus set the stage for the final expulsion of the Confederates from the region.

During the spring of 1864, Sherman's fortunes rose as his friend and commander, Grant, moved up the ladder of military command. When Grant took supreme command of the Western armies, Sherman became commander of the Army of the Tennessee. Then, when Lincoln appointed Grant general-in-chief of all Union armies, Sherman took over Grant's former command in the West. From this position, Sherman launched his Atlanta campaign in April 1864.

Sherman's first objective, as defined by Grant, was to destroy Joseph E. Johnston's army and then to capture the Confederacy's last major rail center at Atlanta. However, when Johnston's army proved both more elusive and more tenacious than Sherman expected, Sherman decided to take a different approach: he would destroy not the army, but the South itself. With about 100,000 men, Sherman descended through Georgia on his way to Atlanta, decimating Confederate supply lines and property along the way. He arrived near Atlanta on July 17 and, after several battles in and around the city during the following six weeks, finally took the last bastion of Confederate strength by forcing General John Bell Hood to evacuate Southern troops on September 1.

After being promoted to major general for his victory, Sherman evacuated the civilian population from Atlanta and commenced to destroy the city's military resources. During his efforts there, a fire was started—most likely by civilians—that eventually gutted a large section of Georgia's capital. After abandoning the city, Sherman sent about 30,000 troops to defend Tennessee and took the rest southward on his famous March to the Sea. Along the way, he and his men set fire to crops and plantation homes, cut every conceivable supply line, and in doing so, crushed whatever spirit the exhausted Confederates had left. Turning north to attempt another offensive against the elusive Johnston in North Carolina, Sherman had arrived near Richmond in time to reinforce Grant in his final encounter with Robert E. Lee.

Five days after Lee surrendered at Appomattox Court House on April 9, 1865, Johnston sent a message asking Sherman to define his terms of surrender. Sherman's unauthorized reply on April 17 caused some controversy. For a man who pursued war with such violence, Sherman's terms were quite benevolent, at least in part because he believed Abraham Lincoln, who had been assassinated just two days before, had not wanted the South to be punished. Called a traitor by War Department chief William Stanton, Sherman was ordered by President Andrew Johnson to renegotiate for stiffer terms.

His extraordinary service during the war more than made up for this gaffe, however, and Sherman continued to serve the military with distinction following the war. He first served as commander of the Division of the Mississippi; in July 1866, he was promoted to lieutenant general. On the election of General Grant to the presidency in 1869, Sherman succeeded him as general-in-chief in Washington, D.C. He served at that post for 14 years, until November 1, 1883. He formally retired from the military on February 8, 1884; he died on February 14, 1891.

Sickles, Daniel
1819(25?)–1914

Had he not lost a leg during his controversial Gettysburg advance, the New York-born Union general might have been court-martialed rather than given the Medal of Honor. A shameless womanizer and shady attorney indicted three times for legal improprieties, Sickles was already a notorious figure before the Civil War. His Tammany Hall political connections got him a seat in the U.S. Congress in 1857, and two years later, he caused the most sensational scandal of the day when he shot and killed his wife's lover—the son of Francis Scott Key—in the streets of Washington, D.C. Defended by Edwin Stanton in a shocking trial, he became the first American acquitted on a murder charge for reason of temporary insanity. Public support for Sickles subsided, however, when he took back his adulterous wife.

Facing a serious setback to his political career, he turned to the military when the war began and raised a rowdy brigade of New Yorkers. Sickles proved a surprisingly adept and stalwart officer in the field. A favorite of his commander, Joseph Hooker, he received several promotions, leading his brigade in the Peninsula campaign, a division at Antietam and Fredericksburg, and a corps at Chancellorsville. Sickles remained a corps commander after Hooker was replaced by George Gordon Meade, who was far less enamored of him.

General Daniel E. Sickles

Still, at Gettysburg, Meade gave Sickles the important assignment of covering the Union's left. On the second day of the July 1863 battle, Sickles decided that his position was vulnerable and, against orders, had his men advance to higher ground a half mile in front of the Federal line. Separated from the rest of the army, Sickles' troops were even more exposed, and the movement left a big gap in the Union's defenses. A furious Meade ordered the maverick general to return to his former position, but by then James Longstreet's Confederate corps had started to charge. As the advantage seesawed back and forth, Sickles' and Longstreet's troops fought savagely over patches of terrain that have become famous in Civil War lore—the Peach Orchard, the Wheatfield, the Devil's Den. His leg shattered by an enemy bullet, Sickles was carried away from the field calmly smoking a cigar, and the limb was amputated within a half hour.

Meanwhile, his troops were driven back and other Federal generals had difficulty plugging the breach he had created in the line, but the Union's left flank did hold. Some have since suggested that Sickles' advance might actually have helped shield the Union defenses from the full fury of Longstreet's assault. But the Gettysburg debacle damaged Sickles military reputation—the Medal of Honor would not be awarded for three more decades—and his persistent criticism of Meade did not help. Although he remained in the army, Sickles was removed from field command.

After the war, he served as military governor of the Carolinas until Andrew Johnson fired him over his harsh Reconstruction policies. Sickles then reentered politics when he was appointed minister to Spain. He returned to Congress in the 1890s and was said to make several visits to the severed leg he lost at Gettysburg, which was exhibited at the Washington, D.C., Army Medical Museum.

Stuart, James Ewell Brown (Jeb)
1833–1864

"We must substitute *esprit* for numbers," Jeb Stuart told his commander, Robert E. Lee. "Therefore I strive to inculcate in my men the spirit of the chase." More than a bit of a show-off in his colorful uniform and long, flowing beard, the Confederate army's best cavalry commander was both a fearless horseman who took incredible risks and a fine soldier who understood strategy and instilled confidence and loyalty in his men.

Deeply religious and, much like his friend Thomas "Stonewall" Jackson, pious and sober in his personal habits, Stuart also had a bit of a wild streak and was prone to both vanity and exhibitionism. However contradictory his personality, however, his skills as a cavalry commander were rarely questioned. Robert E. Lee depended on Stuart's excellent abilities as a scout and a raider throughout the first three years of the war, often referring to him as "the eyes and ears of my army."

Stuart was born and raised in Virginia. He entered West Point in 1850 and graduated thirteenth in his class. Brevetted second lieutenant in the Mounted Rifles, he served on the Texas frontier until he was promoted to first lieutenant on December 20, 1855. The following year, he and his regiment were sent to control the border wars in Kansas; in 1857, Stuart was seriously wounded while fighting the Cheyenne. A part-time inventor, Stuart took time during his recuperation to devise a sabre attachment for the War Department. While in Washington, he volunteered to serve on Robert E. Lee's staff during his mission to capture John Brown after the Harpers Ferry Raid in 1859. Stuart then returned to his regiment in Kansas until his home state of Virginia seceded in April 1861.

Committed to the Confederate cause and to the defense of his home state, Stuart resigned from the U.S. Army and returned to Virginia about a month later. He was commissioned lieutenant colonel of the Virginia Infantry on May 10, 1861, and 13 days later was named captain of the cavalry. At First Bull Run, Stuart's division defended the Confederate left, then performed a sweeping charge upon the rear of the defeated and retreating army. For his actions at Bull Run, he was appointed brigadier general on September 24, 1861, and spent the next several months skirmishing with Federal troops in the Shenandoah Valley.

His talents as a diligent scout and a daring raider were on display during the Peninsula campaign in June 1862. Ordered by Lee to reconnoiter the right flank and rear of George B. McClellan's position along the Chickahominy before the Battle of Mechanicsville, Stuart took 1,000 troops and, going far above and beyond his duty, rode completely around the Union army. Along the more than 150-mile route, he and his men, including the soon-to-

Brigadier General J.E.B. Stuart

be-infamous John Mosby, destroyed considerable Union property and captured dozens of Union soldiers.

Despite the fact that his actions alerted McClellan to a possible Confederate attack and allowed the Union general time to prepare, the information and pillage he brought back to Richmond earned him a hero's welcome from Lee. Stuart continued to reconnoiter McClellan's army as it made its retreat during the seven days battles. On July 25, 1862, Stuart was promoted to major general and put in command of all cavalry forces in the Army of Northern Virginia.

Just before the Battle of Second Bull Run, Stuart performed an outrageous, but successful, raid on John Pope's headquarters at Catlett's Station. Covering 60 miles in just 26

hours, Stuart returned with two guns, 1,500 men, and a coat that contained a notebook outlining the disposition of Federal troops. These orders gave Lee vital information that helped him win at Second Bull Run on September 1, 1862. Thanks to this victory, Lee dared to risk an invasion of Maryland soon after and ordered Stuart to lead the advance of Jackson's corps while Jackson rode to Harpers Ferry.

It was good-humored and dedicated Jeb Stuart who was forced to tell Lee that a copy of Lee's battle orders had been appropriated by Union troops, thereby placing the whole campaign in jeopardy. The result was the bloody battle of Antietam on September 17, 1862, during which Stuart and his cavalry fought valiantly to hold the vital gap of the South Mountain. As Lee retreated into Virginia following the battle, Stuart rode north to attempt to cut a Union supply line in Chambersburg, Pennsylvania. Although he failed in that effort, he and his 1,800 men managed to ride 126 miles in just three days, circling McClellan's army again. Along the way, they destroyed a machine shop, raided several private stores, and captured about 500 horses before recrossing the Potomac on October 12.

At the Battle of Fredericksburg two months later, Stuart's cavalry guarded the extreme right of the Confederate line throughout this surprise Confederate victory. During the following winter and spring, Stuart was able to give Lee information on Joseph Hooker's crossing of the Rappahannock River in time for Lee to prepare a brilliant strategy for the Battle of Chancellorsville on May 3, 1863. Stuart's cavalry also controlled all of the roads around Chancellorsville, keeping Hooker from discerning the Confederate position. When Stonewall Jackson was killed and his second-in-command, Ambrose P. Hill, was wounded during the battle itself, Stuart ably took command of Jackson's corps.

Following the spectacular Confederate win at Chancellorsville, Lee planned another Northern invasion, and once again counted on Stuart to provide reconnaissance. On June 9, 1863, he and his men encountered a Union cavalry patrol and there ensued the Battle of Brandy Station, Virginia, the largest cavalry engagement in American history and one that brought Stuart another victory. His next endeavor, however, was less than successful.

To prepare for the Battle of Gettysburg, Lee sent Stuart out on another scouting mission to locate and report on Union troop movements. As was his habit, Stuart decided to push forward and take another "ride around McClellan." The Federal army, however, occupied much more ground and was much more active than Stuart had assumed. Driven far to the east, the "eyes and ears" of Lee's army was out of touch with his commander for more than 10 days. At least part of the blame for the devastating Confederate defeat belongs to Stuart, who did not arrive on the field until the second day of battle. Apparently learning his lesson, Stuart stayed in close contact with Lee during the next few months as he tracked Grant's movements during the devastating Wilderness campaign.

After the vicious Battle of Spotsylvania, Philip H. Sheridan, the Union cavalry leader, and 12,000 cavalry began moving toward Richmond with Stuart following in close pursuit with 4,500 exhausted men. They met in

the Wilderness at a place called Yellow Tavern. During a desperate charge, Stuart was mortally wounded. He was immediately taken to Richmond, but died the following day on May 12, 1864. The personal and military loss to Lee and to the Army of Northern Virginia was incalculable.

Thomas, George Henry
1816–1870

Earning his famous nickname "The Rock of Chickamauga" for steadfastly holding his position during the Georgia battle after most of the Federal troops had been wiped from the field, the Virginia-born Union general proved to be one of the North's greatest military assets.

Thomas' gutsy boyhood ride to warn isolated neighbors of Nat Turner's slave uprising helped him win an appointment to West Point. Becoming an artillery and cavalry instructor at his alma mater, he also fought in the Mexican War and served with the famous 2nd Cavalry alongside future battlefield opponents John Bell Hood and Albert Sidney Johnston. Although Thomas was physically as rock-solid as his future nickname would suggest, an 1860 frontier wound almost ended his army career.

But at the outbreak of the Civil War, he returned to active duty—remaining with the Union, however, to the disgust of Confederate family members and colleagues and the suspicion of some among the North's high command. Initially stationed in Virginia, Thomas was transferred west, where he brought the Confederacy one of its first defeats near Mill Springs, Kentucky, in January 1862, routing a small force under A. S. Johnston.

After a solid performance at Perryville in October, he refused an order to take over the command of his superior Don Carlos Buell. Thomas remained Buell's ranking officer in the New Years' 1863 Battle of Murfreesboro, where he stolidly protected the Union center. In a still more dazzling display of his matchless defensive skills, he made his legendary stand at Chickamauga in September, rallying his troops to hold their ground at Snodgrass Hill for hours after Union commander William Rosecrans had retreated. Thomas finally ordered a withdrawal at dusk, saving the Union force from destruction.

Rewarding him with the command of the Army of the Cumberland, Ulysses S. Grant did not want to assign a primary role to Thomas' troops in the following month's actions at Chattanooga, thinking they were still too demoralized from the earlier engagement. Thomas and his men were eager to prove otherwise and, ordered merely to make a limited assault on the Confederate line at the base of Missionary Ridge, sent an attack force of 23,000 that had little trouble overrunning the enemy trenches. Lacking further instructions, the exhilarated troops continued up the slope and swept the Confederates off the ridge altogether, winning a stunning victory and avenging their loss at Chickamauga. Thomas' army provided less dramatic but still invaluable support for William T. Sherman's advance on Atlanta in 1864.

Later in the year, he was sent back to Tennessee to challenge John Bell Hood's desperate attempt to retake the eastern portion of the state. Assembling a force of over 60,000 outside Nashville in his characteristically calm and methodical fashion, Thomas ignored Grant's insistent orders to attack immediately. He was about to be relieved of command when he finally launched his offense on December 16, an overwhelming assault that all but annihilated Hood's army.

With Thomas' conclusive victory, the Confederate military was essentially finished in the West. Thomas remained in the Regular army at the war's conclusion, serving as commander of the Military Division of the Pacific when he died.

Toombs, Robert Augustus
1810–1885

After resigning his Georgia Senate seat following the election of Abraham Lincoln, Robert Toombs stormed out of the Senate chamber, demanded from the bursar his salary due plus mileage back to Georgia, and went home to organize secession in his state. Brilliant but unpredictable, Toombs would serve not only as Jefferson Davis' secretary of state, but as brigadier general in the Confederate army.

One of the wealthiest planters and most powerful politicians in Georgia, Toombs received his education at the University of Georgia and Union College, New York, then went on to become a lawyer. He became a state legislator in 1837, serving there for six years, after which he went to the United States House of Representatives from 1844 to 1852, then won election to the U.S. Senate. Throughout his early career, Toombs, like many of his fellow Southerners, was anxious to effect a compromise between North and South that would maintain the Union. In this respect, he was aligned most closely with colleagues Howell Cobb and Alexander Stephens.

Like many Southerners, however, Toombs saw the election of Republican Abraham Lincoln as a sign that compromise was no longer possible and strongly urged Georgia to secede. In February 1861, he was sent as a delegate to the Montgomery convention and lobbied hard to be elected to a high office, preferably to the presidency. With several powerful Georgian candidates, including Cobb and Stephens, splitting the vote, Toombs lost out to Jefferson Davis.

Bitterly disappointed, he nearly refused appointment to secretary of state. After initially urging restraint at Fort Sumter, Toombs became an ardent supporter of all-out war once the first shots had been fired. It quickly became clear to both Toombs and the president that the State Department was not the place for him. His restless energy found little outlet in the department, especially since the Confederacy was not yet recognized by any foreign power, nor would it ever be.

On July 24, 1861, Toombs resigned his cabinet post to take a more active, and certainly more exciting, role on the battlefield. Despite the fact that he had no military training, he asked Davis to appoint him as brigadier general; Davis, with misgivings, obliged. Toombs first saw battle during the Seven Days campaign, where he fought aggressively but unwisely. At White Oak Swamp, he took it upon himself to convert a minor military demonstration into a full-scale assault on the heavily-manned Federal entrenchments and was repulsed with a great loss of men.

Later in the campaign, he was arrested for allowing his troops to leave their posts without first gaining permission from his own commander to do so. This breach of duty caused him to lose his command for several weeks, until Second Bull Run. His careless disregard of military tack caused Toombs to be loathed by most of his men and passed over for promotion by his superiors. Although he fought well at Antietam, where 550 men under his command successfully challenged more than 20 times their number, he was disappointed at his lack of advancement and chafed under military rules and regulations. Mary Chesnut wrote in her diary: "Toombs is ready for a revolution. He curses freely everything Confederate from a president to a horse boy and thinks there is a conspiracy against him in the army." He finally resigned his commission on March 3, 1863, and returned to Georgia, where he remained an unrelenting critic of the Davis administration.

He returned to uniform just once, joining the militia to oppose William Tecumseh Sherman during his devastating March through Georgia. Barely escaping arrest at the war's end, Toombs fled to Cuba and Europe, returning to Georgia in 1867. Because he refused to apply for a pardon, however, he was unable to hold public office. He died in Washington, Georgia, on December 15, 1885.

Watie, Stand
1806–1871

The highest ranking Native American in either force, the Cherokee leader was the last Confederate general to surrender—more than two months after Appomattox.

Watie was born in Georgia, educated in Connecticut, and became a prominent planter and journalist. He was also instrumental in negotiating the controversial 1835 treaty with the United States that relocated the Cherokee Nation from the Southeast to the Indian Territory (present-day Oklahoma). An early supporter of the Confederacy, Watie raised a pro-secession home guard as the Civil War commenced. It was an unofficial command, for the Cherokees initially intended to remain neutral in the conflict, despite the fact that many of the more affluent owned black slaves. The Confederacy, however, eager to protect its vulnerable Western border and hoping to gain as many as 20,000 new army recruits, sought the support of the Indian Territory tribes. Promised better treatment than it had received from the federal government and guaranteed rights long denied, the Cherokee Nation entered into an alliance with the South in 1861.

Watie, a principal backer of the bargain, entered the Confederate military later in the year and was appointed colonel of the "Cherokee Mounted Rifles." The Southern armies attracted far fewer Indian troops than had first been envisioned, and many of the several thousand who did enlist, frustrated at being kept poorly supplied, soon abandoned the cause. Watie and his cavalry, however, served throughout the war.

After participating in the fighting at Wilson's Creek, Missouri, in August 1861, they distinguished themselves the following March during the Battle of Pea Ridge, Arkansas, in a bold charge on a federal artillery battery. With the Union occupation of the Indian Territories in 1863, most of Watie's subsequent Civil War service involved local raids and skirmishes, frequently vying against pro-North Native American units.

That same year, the Cherokee Nation repudiated its treaty with the Confederacy and allied with the Union, while Watie continued to lead a large pro-South faction, his battalion also including Creek, Seminole, and Osage troops. Promoted to brigadier general in May 1864, he gained a reputation as an expert guerrilla fighter for such successful actions as the capture of a Union steamship on the Arkansas River carrying a cargo worth over $100,000. The Northern press paid great attention to these forays, printing highly exaggerated accounts of atrocities the Indians allegedly committed against the Union boys. As the North's victory was assured in 1865, Watie proved to be the Confederate general most reluctant to accept defeat. Lee and Johnston had surrendered in the East in April; even headstrong Department of the Trans-Mississippi commander E. Kirby Smith capitulated the following month.

But Watie did not give up until four weeks

later, finally surrendering at Doaksville on June 23, 1865. His own fight lasting months longer than the Civil War, he went back to planting and the tobacco business.

Wheeler, Joseph
1836–1906

"Fighting Joe" Wheeler was a man to whom the ordinary rarely applied. Born of New England parents who migrated to Augusta, Georgia, before Wheeler's birth, he is nevertheless remembered as one of the Confederacy's finest cavalry commanders. More, he is one of the few generals to whom Robert E. Lee gave the term outstanding. Graduating from West Point in 1859 with high standings in military subjects and poor standings in academics, Wheeler spent two years fighting Indians in New Mexico before his native state seceded from the Union; on April 22, 1861, he resigned his U.S. commission and offered his sword to his new country.

At first commissioned anew as a first lieutenant in the Confederate Regular army, Wheeler very soon received a post and promotion to colonel of the 19th Alabama Infantry; he led this regiment in the bloody fighting at Shiloh, received an infantry brigade very soon after—and on the heels of that assignment, Wheeler suddenly found himself in command of the cavalry in the Army of Mississippi. By the end of the war, Wheeler had risen successively through the ranks to finish as a lieutenant general, but he always retained command of the cavalry in the Western theater of the war.

There is almost no action in the West that Wheeler was not somehow a part of. At Murfreesboro and Chickamauga, he was instrumental in keeping the commanders of the army aware of Federal maneuvers. He was heavily engaged in the Knoxville campaign and was a constant thorn in the side of William T. Sherman throughout the Atlanta campaign. Wheeler's men were effectively the only troops to have any success in the attempt to contain Sherman's March to the Sea. His cavalrymen, known to the Federal enemy as "Wheeler's Raiders," were feared by opponents far more thoroughly armed and better sup-

Lieutenant General Joseph Wheeler

plied than he, and right up to the end, his very name caused the upset of many a Federal commander's equilibrium.

Before the surrender of Joseph Johnston, Wheeler's men broke away and, to their discredit, were involved in less than admirable excesses against isolated groups of Federal soldiers in the closing days of the war. But even that could not diminish the fame of their young commander, who had, it was said, participated in over 800 skirmishes, 200 engagements, and had been wounded three times in the course of the war's four years.

After the war, Wheeler settled into what must have seemed a rather commonplace life. He married and relocated to a town in Alabama that was instituted and named in his honor. He planted cotton and practiced law, until Reconstruction ended and politics became a major interest in his life. In 1881, he initially won election to the Forty-seventh Congress, but the election was contested; in the end, his seat was taken by a Mr. Lowe. Before the end of the term, however, Lowe died—and Wheeler was elected to take his place. He was also a member of the Forty-ninth Congress, involved in military and fiscal policy-making, to no one's surprise. He became the senior Democrat on the House Ways and Means Committee, and in a show of "no hard feelings" was involved in the revocation of the harsher sentences of Union General Fitz-John Porter's court-martial decision. For the most part, however, Wheeler was known as a man whose interests primarily lay with his own people. Everything he did, even his work toward the continuing reconciliation between North and South, he did for Alabama.

Such a career would have been enough for an ordinary man, but Wheeler was hardly ordinary. When the Spanish-American War flared in the 1890s, Wheeler was appointed a major general in command of Volunteers, one of three Confederate cavalry generals to serve in this war; he commanded a cavalry division in the Santiago Expedition, was present at the landing at Daiquiri, Cuba, and started the fighting at Las Guasimas in 1898. He was present at the Battle of San Juan Hill on July 1, 1898, though illness prevented him from participating. Recovering in time to join the siege of Santiago, Wheeler figures prominently in reports of the action. Ever busy, Wheeler was in charge of the convalescent camp in Montauk Point, Long Island, when the wounded of the war were returned to the United States; he was then given a brigade of cavalry in the Philippines. On July 16, 1900, he was appointed a brigadier general in the U.S. Army, and finally retired three months later at the age of 64. Wheeler was an ardent writer and champion of the South; he wrote an innovative cavalry tactics manual during the Civil War, as well as articles concerning the operations of his Confederate troopers, and his interests in genealogy are evidenced by a book he coauthored with his wife on the ancestry of their children.

Wheeler lived out the remainder of his life in peace and quiet, passing away in Brooklyn, New York, in 1906. He is buried in Arlington National Cemetery, Arlington, Virginia.

★ ★ ★